Angelo Beolco (Il Ruzante)

Twayne's World Authors Series
Italian Literature

Anthony Oldcorn, Editor

Brown University

TWAS 815

ANGELVS BEOLCVS CIVIS PATAVINVS
COGNOMENTO RVZATES

ANGELO BEOLCO (IL RUZANTE)
By permission of the Folger Shakespeare Library.

Angelo Beolco (Il Ruzante)

By Linda L. Carroll

Newcomb College, Tulane University

Twayne Publishers
A Division of G. K. Hall & Co. • *Boston*

Angelo Beolco (Il Ruzante)
Linda L. Carroll

Copyright 1990 by G. K. Hall & Co.
All rights reserved.
Published by Twayne Publishers
A Division of G. K. Hall & Co.
70 Lincoln Street
Boston, Massachusetts 02111

Copyediting supervised by Barbara Sutton
Book production by Gabrielle B. McDonald
Book design by Barbara Anderson

Typeset in 11 pt. Garamond
by Compositors Corporation, Cedar Rapids, Iowa

Printed on permanent/durable acid-free paper
and bound in the United States of America

First published, 1990
10 9 8 7 6 5 4 3 2 1

Library of Congress Cataloging-in-Publication Data

Carroll, Linda L.
    Angelo Beolco (Il Ruzante) / by Linda L. Carroll.
        p.   cm. — (Twayne's world authors series ; TWAS 815. Italian
    literature)
    Includes bibliographical references.
    ISBN 0-8057-8255-9 (alk. paper)
    1. Ruzante, 1502?–1542—Criticism and interpretation.   I. Title.
    II. Series: Twayne's world authors series ; TWAS 815.   III. Series:
    Twayne's world authors series. Italian literature.
    PQ4610.B47Z6   1990
    852'.3—dc20   89-38925
                                                                    CIP

*to Ed
and to Branwen*

Contents

About the Author

Linda L. Carroll is associate professor of Italian at Newcomb College, Tulane University. A native of Seattle, she received her A.B. from Princeton University and her M.A. and Ph.D. from Harvard University. She has received grants from the Gonzaga Research Council, Fulbright Commission, National Endowment for the Humanities, Delmas Foundation, and Newberry Library. A former member of the Board of Trustees of the Washington Association of Foreign Language Teachers, she has been included in the *Directory of American Scholars, Directory of International Biography, Who's Who in the West,* and *World Who's Who of Women.* The author of *Language and Dialect in Ruzante and Goldoni* (Ravenna: Longo, 1981) and numerous articles and reviews on Renaissance popular theater, Professor Carroll is currently preparing a monograph on popular theater and politics in Renaissance Venice and a translation of Beolco's plays.

Preface

As Angelo Beolco stated throughout his stage career, his primary concern was the incorporation of the lowly and their forms of expression into the social and literary canons. Using the space that Carnival theater apportioned to the marginal, he created and played a peasant character, Ruzante, who used humor to tear down aristocratic literature and society, replacing them with a world of shared humanity that he valued more than book learning. Ruzante's identity merged so thoroughly with Beolco's own that the playwright signed himself by that name in legal and artistic documents.

Evidence supports the hypothesis that Beolco's break with dominant norms came in response to the pressures exerted upon the upper and lower classes by newly felt economic and political restrictions. The aristocracy was finding that trade, its chief source of income, had been seriously limited, while the concentration of wealth in a few hands had increased the rate of conspicuous consumption necessary to maintaining high status. The peasantry's scope of personal and social authority, meanwhile, was increasingly circumscribed by city dominance, as former merchants turned to agriculture. The natural son of a noble family passing its prime and (probably) of a servant of peasant origin, Beolco was subject to the pressures upon both groups, as well as to the restrictions imposed by the condition of his birth. He expressed his outrage in a series of plays that focused on peasant life, attempting to restructure society by arguing for its validity and for the extension of equal privileges and obligations to all. Perhaps because of the limitations they felt, Venetian aristocrats were sympathetic to Beolco and his views during the tumultuous period after the Cambrai Wars. But when government took a more autocratic turn, and Beolco responded with increasing stridency, he was relegated to lesser mainland circles. Following the playwright's lead, the present study concentrates on his life and historical circumstances, and on the concerns of folk culture, more than on traditional literary and theatrical approaches.

Beolco's polemic put him in the company of a small number of Renaissance women and men who anticipated the movement of Western culture toward democracy. His work, in fact, was not widely appreciated until the nineteenth and twentieth centuries, after reforms had extended cultural and political participation to the majority of the population. Aristocratic and democratic strains exist even in Beolco scholarship. Some scholars attempt to incorporate him into the authorizing system by linking him with the texts and patrons of high culture. Others recognize his pioneering spirit, demonstrating how he used such resources to his own ends. The present writer is persuaded that the latter approach more accurately reflects the playwright and his works.

I acknowledge with gratitude the contribution made to the present study by the work of other Beolco scholars and of academic colleagues. I also wish to thank the institutions without whose generous support it could not have been carried out: the Gonzaga Research Council, the Fulbright Commission, the National Endowment for the Humanities, and the Gladys Krieble Delmas Foundation. Giulio Einaudi Editore has graciously permitted extensive quotations from the Zorzi edition of the plays. The portrait of Beolco on the frontispiece is reproduced with the kind permission of the Folger Shakespeare Library. Ronald Mason, Joseph Bosco and Michael Gerli deserve special recognition for their assistance. And, most of all, I am grateful to my husband, Ed, for his unfaltering and indispensable support.

Linda L. Carroll

Newcomb College, Tulane University

Chronology

Question marks indicate a lack of reliable information about one or more items (date, place, identity of play, etc.). Consult the section on the dates, manuscripts, and performances of each play for details.

1496 Angelo Beolco born in Padua (?)

1509–1517 Wars of Cambrai and Venetian reconquest of mainland; collected material for plays and wrote early versions of *Betia* (?) and *The Veteran* (?)

1517 *Pastoral* (?); performance: *Pastoral* in Padua (?)

1520 Performances: *Pastoral* (?) in Venice

1521 *First Oration;* performance: *First Oration* at Asolo; first contact with Alvise Cornaro

1522 *Playful Letter* (?); early version of *The Woman from Ancona* (?); performance(s): *Playful Letter* (?), early version of *The Woman from Ancona* (?) in Venice

1523 Correr version of *Betia* (?); performances: Correr *Betia* (?) in Venice at Carnival and at wedding of Doge's grandson; Grimani dies; Gritti elected Doge

1524 Performance: *Playful Letter* (?) in Venice; father's death (?)

1525 Performances: *Betia* (?) and second play in Venice; joins Cornaro's household

1526 Performance in Venice at dinner insulting to France; receives severance sum from father's estate; buys expensive horse; marries Giustina Palatino (?)

after 1526 Marciana version of *Betia;* formation of (semi) professional acting troupe

1527 Buys second expensive horse; exhausts severance sum

1528 Marciana version of *Moscheta* (?); *Second Oration;* performances: Marciana version of *Moscheta* at Ferrara (?); *Second Oration* at Asolo; acquires land of famine-ridden peasants for Cornaro

1529 *Witty Dialogue;* Veronese prologue of *Moscheta* (?); *The Vet-*

eran (?); performances: *Witty Dialogue* at Fosson and Ferrara (?) in January; *Moscheta* (?), Veronese prologue (?), and *The Veteran* (?) at Ferrara in May (?); acquires land of famine-ridden peasants for Cornaro; Cornaro named administrator of bishopric of Padua

1530   *Weasel* (?)

1531   *Flora's Play* (?); performance in Padua (?): *Flora's Play* (?)

1532   *The Girl from Piove* (?); printed version of *Moscheta* (?); performances: *The Girl from Piove* (?) at Ferrara, final version of *Moscheta* (?) or *The Girl from Piove* (?) in Padua

1533   *The Cow Comedy;* performances: *The Cow Comedy* and *The Girl from Piove* (?) in Padua; petition to Venetian Senate for printing rights to *The Cow Comedy* and *The Girl from Piove*

after 1533   Becomes involved in land management

1534   Performance: final version of *The Woman from Ancona* (?) in Padua (?)

1535   Given power of attorney for half brother Lazzaro for division of father's estate

1536   *Letter to Alvarotto;* given power of attorney for half brother Ludovico, in prison in Venice

1539   Given power of attorney for half brother Pietro, living in banishment in Ferrara

1540   Divides father's estate among half brothers

1542   Prepares Sperone Speroni's *Canace* for performance in Padua; dies in Padua and is buried in Church of San Daniele

Chapter One
Family Background and Early Life

Family Origins

The noble Beolcos originated in Milan, possibly taking their name from Castel Beolco, near which they owned large amounts of land.[1] The family, whose members distinguished themselves as courtiers, soldiers, and officials, achieved even greater political status in the fifteenth century. Pietro Beolco sat on the general council of Milan, while his son Giovanni held the office of chief of police (*questore*) and made significant loans to Duke Ludovico Sforza, the city's despot. Giovanni's brother Lazzaro migrated to the eastern Po Valley after the Peace of Lodi (1454) had quelled the wars between Venice and Milan. He and the other Milanese merchants who acted similarly were perhaps responding to the pressures exerted by a population increase that particularly affected the patrician class and that social and economic structures, reduced by a century of Black Death, were unable to accommodate.

Lazzaro opened profitable dry goods shops in Vicenza and Padua.[2] Around 1460 he married Paola, whose father's recent success in the cloth trade had brought her family to Padua from the nearby village of Pernumia. Their eldest child, Giovanni Francesco (Angelo's father), was probably born there in 1461. In the same year, Lazzaro moved to Venice, where he would live near the Rialto (Venice's main commercial district) and possibly keep a shop. He occasionally commuted to Padua, staying with his sons when they were older. Vicentine citizenship, a status that allowed a merchant to transport goods freely to Venice, was apparently conferred on Lazzaro by 1464, and in 1473 he and his descendants were formally declared Paduan citizens. Such an achievement testifies to his acumen: mainland cities were reluctant to incorporate outsiders, fearing that they were more interested in citizenship's privileges than its duties.

The new printing industry also figured among Lazzaro's commercial interests.[3] He underwrote an edition of Plutarch's *Lives,* rented out a printing press, sold books, and loaned money to a professor and to printers. The Mil-

anese merchant maintained other personal and commercial contacts with the
University that would bear fruit in the lives of his descendants, as historian
Paolo Sambin has noted.

Eventually, Giovanni Francesco and his younger brother Giovanni Jacopo
enrolled as students at the University of Padua, living together in a house
rented by their father.[4] Some trouble must have arisen, however. Lazzaro sent
his eldest son to live with an uncle, but the headstrong Giovanni Francesco
ran away the next day. Determined to study the new classical learning, he
pawned some family valuables he had pilfered and, having bought a horse
with the proceeds, set off for Florence, humanism's center. However, he was
prevented from entering the city by the lack of proper documents. Afraid of
crossing war-torn Tuscany to the other university at Pisa, he reluctantly returned home.

Resuming his studies in Padua, Giovanni Francesco obtained a doctorate
in arts in 1485, a year after Lazzaro's early death.[5] He initiated a university
career and, with his brother and other relatives, conducted numerous commercial ventures in Milan, Venice, and Padua.

Illegitimate Birth and Youth

The turbulence evident in Giovanni Francesco's flight manifested itself
again in about 1496 when an illegitimate son, Angelo, was born to him.[6]
Angelo's mother appears to have been the servant Maria, brought into the
Beolco household about ten years earlier at age thirteen. Perhaps as a result of
Angelo's birth, Paola seems to have become more strict with her servants and
her no-longer-young son. She apparently fired Maria when her contract ex-
pired in 1497; within a few years Giovanni Francesco took minor orders and
married, buying a large town house in Padua that would remain the family
seat.[7] The trend toward stability may have been reinforced by Giovanni
Francesco's wife, Francesca di Berto de Guidotti da Montagnana, and by his
election as the *priore* (head) of the faculty of medicine and arts in 1500.

Maria, who came from Padua's semirural outskirts, appears to have served
as the model for the lusty peasant woman who recurs in all of Beolco's plays.
When she left the Beolco family, Angelo would have been about a year old.
Nancy Dersofi sees Beolco's work as recreating "the lost pastoral idyll of the
peasant."[8] One could take this hypothesis a step further by interpreting the
lost idyll specifically as the playwright's abruptly terminated early life with
his mother.

Illegitimacy was not an unusual condition in the Renaissance, even in the
highest social circles. Venetian nobleman Andrea Gritti fathered an illegiti-

mate family when he was a merchant in Constantinople, which, while the subject of complaints during his campaign for the dogeship in 1523, did not prevent his election. Pietro Bembo, the well-known exponent of Neoplatonic love, barred from marrying by his priestly status, lived with a woman who bore him three children.[9] Nor was illegitimacy unusual in the Beolco family. Lazzaro's illegitimate son Melchiorre fathered two sons, one of whom was illegitimate; the legitimate son produced an illegitimate daughter.

While common, such a status became problematic for the child by the early sixteenth century, when an aristocracy defined by proper birth dominated the public sphere. As aristocrats lost power to the nation-states that were invading and conquering Italy, a psychology of defeat led them to reinforce their control over local society as a means of restoring their lost sense of importance.[10] Part of that dominance was the formulation of a series of distinctions that separated the powerful from the unpowerful, the pure from the impure, the legitimate from the illegitimate.

The stress on legitimacy also served an economic function. Venetian patricians were removing themselves from commercial activities interrupted by Turkish wars and Portuguese competition, and becoming landed squires or living off invested income. Economic difficulties are summarized by Ugo Tucci: "The problem for the rich was not so much one of further growth as of the conservation and management of what was left."[11] Faced with such restrictions, the aristocracy limited the number of heirs by controlling marriages and refusing to recognize illegitimate offspring.

Illegitimate sons of aristocratic families were thus prevented from enjoying the economic and political privileges of their siblings. They could not participate in the governance of the state, a loss not to be underestimated in a culture that accorded the highest importance to civic life. Only those specifically named in wills could inherit, and even then were often limited to nominal sums.[12] Illegitimate brothers were excluded from commercial ventures subsidized by the patrimony and were frequently denied professional preparation. Though born and often raised in the houses of their noble fathers, illegitimate sons (or natural sons, as they were called) were confined to the humble status of artisans and craftsmen, while their brothers became gentlemen, the highest of Renaissance social conditions.

The case of Melchiorre Beolco, Angelo's illegitimate uncle, is a typical one. His two legitimate brothers jointly used their inheritance to underwrite various business schemes and buy a large house and farmland. Melchiorre, excluded from his father's and aunt's wills, is reported only as living and keeping his shop in the family house.[13] Moreover, he was often asked by his half brothers to manage their investments although he would not profit from his work. Both legitimate brothers studied at the university, while Melchiorre went into trade. His incorporation into the wool guild in 1504 indicated that he was not considered an aristocrat.[14]

Although Melchiorre included his illegitimate granddaughter (who may have been an infant at the time) in his will, he omitted his illegitimate son Imperio and left his possessions to his legitimate son Giulio, or, in the absence of heirs, to Giovanni Jacopo's legitimate son Lazzaro. No other member of the family left legacies to illegitimate offspring during this period (with a minor exception in the cases of Angelo and Imperio, discussed below).[15] One wonders if illegitimate cousins Imperio and Angelo fathered no children because of the difficulties that their own births created for them.

Illegitimates were also excluded from the tradition of ancestral names that bound families together. Melchiorre's name was not familial, though it did perpetuate the Milanese devotion to the Three Wise Men. It and that of his son Giulio were repeated in Giovanni Jacopo's line for one hundred and fifty years, to its extinction. A different situation held for Imperio (discussed below) and Angelo, whose names are not connected with the Beolco family and were not perpetuated by descendants, facts consistent with Giovanni Francesco's conservatism in the matter.[16] Indeed, Angelo (Angel) like Diodato (God-given) is a name commonly given to illegitimate children. It is not to be excluded that Angelo's name was chosen by his mother; a local devotion is indicated by the existence of two towns of that name in the vicinity of Padua. In later life, Angelo would be the administrator of the church in one of them, Sant'Angelo di Piove di Sacco, and base a play on the lives of refugees from the region around it.

Padua Rebels

The next event to affect the Beolco family would also permanently scar the Venetian Republic and its fortunes.[17] Frightened by Venice's century-long success in subjugating its hinterland, a group of European powers including France, the Holy Roman Empire, Mantua, Ferrara, the Papacy, and Spain signed a pact in late 1508. Called the League of Cambrai, the alliance had as its secret purpose the division of Venetian holdings among its members. The areas north and west of Venice (including Padua) were to be apportioned to the Emperor, with whom they had maintained their traditional ties. The League's massed forces inflicted upon Venice the most crushing defeat of the city's thousand-year history at Agnadello on 14 May 1509. Its armies routed, Venice lost all its mainland territories. Padua, the dominion's capstone since its conquest in 1405, gave itself over to the Emperor. After the

Venetian governors had left, a makeshift Imperial flag was hoisted over the city to cries of "Imperio! Imperio!"[18]

The republic's forces, led by Andrea Gritti, recaptured the city six weeks later. Venice moved swiftly to stifle the uprising and punish the rebels, whose number included many in the university community and clerics loyal to the Pope. Large numbers of Paduans were arrested and imprisoned there or in Venice, including Giovanni Jacopo and Melchiorre Beolco, and a number of members of the Beolco circle.[19] By the end of the following month, Venice had regained sufficient control for the Venetian governors to order hangings on the spot for some of those still bold enough to consort with the Emperor. The fates of the prisoners taken to Venice were various. Those considered the most responsible, and perhaps capable of rallying the greatest following, were hanged before a crowd in St. Mark's Square.[20] The Beolco brothers did not suffer so grievously. Having convinced the authorities that they were Milanese, they were released from prison in the spring on the condition that they remain in Venice.

In 1511, while Giovanni Jacopo was still under surveillance, he made a series of wills that give a clear indication of Beolco family financial attitudes. While on leave (authorized or not) in Padua, he had the first will drawn up,[21] the chief heirs of which were two religious orders (at the time he was preparing for the priesthood). The only relatives to receive significant sums were his mother Paola, to whom he left an annual income of twenty ducats, and his illegitimate nephew Imperio, who received an annual income of ten ducats. The latter was probably an infant, as his name Imperio with its connections to the Paduan rebellion seems to indicate, and his father Melchiorre was still confined to Venice. Later, apparently at the instigation of his mother, Giovanni Jacopo added a codicil to his will giving her an annual income of forty ducats which, at her death, would pass to Angelo, then about fifteen, previously excluded from the will of her wealthy sister.

The situation favoring Angelo did not last long. After Giovanni Jacopo returned to Venice, he again changed his will. Melchiorre received a small sum and Imperio a small annual income. Giovanni Jacopo named as his universal heirs Giovanni Francesco's two legitimate sons Lazzaro and Pietro; his mother Paola would have the usufruct of his goods during her lifetime.[22] The changes indicate that while in the first two wills Giovanni Jacopo attempted to protect the most vulnerable members of the family from the dangers of war, he soon reverted to the common aristocratic strategy of consolidating the patrimony in the legitimate line. Eventually even the legacies to Melchiorre and Imperio would be eliminated, and all goods would be willed to his legitimate heirs.

The Venetians allowed Melchiorre to return to Padua in January of 1512; within the year, Giovanni Francesco and Giovanni Jacopo had made him one of their business agents.[23] In 1513, a few weeks before he completed a second degree in medicine, Giovanni Francesco withdrew a portion from the joint patrimony and bought four fields near his mother's village of Pernumia, where he would soon take up residence. His decision may have been prompted by financial considerations. The war had damaged the house in Padua and increased the price of farm products. A medical degree would allow him to supplement his income by working as a country doctor. Except for a brief period as prior of the faculty of medicine and arts in the winter of 1513–1514, he spent much of his remaining time tending to the country holdings with a rigorous attention to economic interests evidenced in long contracts detailing the obligations of his peasant renters.

Chapter Two
Early Plays: Entering the World of the Peasant

The *Pastoral:* Challenge to Formalism

Manuscript, Date, and Performances. The irregularity of Angelo Beolco's background appears to have impelled him to write plays questioning the hierarchical values that prevailed in contemporary literature and society. The plays enjoyed a first (and, it would turn out, atypical) success with Venice's dominant élite during the uncertain period that followed the 1516 Treaty of Noyon concluding the Wars of Cambrai. While Venice had succeeded in its supreme effort to reconquer the mainland dominion lost in 1509 and thus had reason to celebrate, it had still suffered long-term damage to both material interests and reputation. The result was a disruption of society sufficient to allow room for Beolco's unconventional proposals.

The dates of Beolco's plays, for many of which only scant circumstantial evidence exists, remain the subject of much critical discussion. The question has assumed more than ordinary importance because of the fluctuation in attitudes toward official culture evident in the works, which has stimulated many critics to theorize about Beolco's evolution as a thinker. The present study thus pays close attention to both the evidence available for the date of each work and the critical interpretations that have been given to it.

Beolco's first known play, the *Pastoral,* exists in a single manuscript bearing the date 1521. It was probably written and originally staged in Padua after the conclusion of the wars, in about 1517, a hypothesis suggested by Alfred Mortier and Mario Baratto, and developed by Giorgio Padoan.[1] It may also have been performed at Beolco's first recorded appearance in Venice (Carnival 1520), having come to the attention of the young Venetian patricians who organized the festivities through their contacts with the University of Padua, which resumed regular classes in 1517.[2]

Venetian Carnival entertainment of the time was lavish, celebrating (and perhaps covering anxiety concerning) the conclusion of the wars. According to Venetian diarist Marin Sanudo, the 1520 performance occurred at a party

7

that lasted all night, and included a pageant, a ball, and a supper. It was
sponsored by the Company of the Immortals, one of the numerous Stocking
Troupes (Compagnie della Calza: named for the fashionable hose their members wore as emblems) that organized aristocratic and state festivities. Three
days later Domenico Trevisan hosted his son's troupe, the Company of the
Gardeners, in his home in the Procuratie, the prestigious government build-
ings in St. Mark's Square, which he occupied as Procurator of St. Mark (one
of the highest offices in Venice). The program included a ball and "the
Paduan peasant comedy, and someone nicknamed Ruzante and someone else
nicknamed Menato did a good job as peasants."[3] As has often been noted,
Beolco was called by his character's name from the outset of his career, as was
his stage companion Marco Alvarotto (Menato).

Stocking Troupes were composed of young Venetian aristocrats, though
prominent nobles from outside the city were sometimes invited to become
members.[4] They planned parties, including the initiation festivities for the
group, elaborate patrician Carnival festivities, members' wedding celebra-
tions, and, occasionally, entertainment for state guests. The large number of
festivities organized, as well as competition for the most unusual spectacle,
led the troupes to invite various nonmembers to entertain, including buf-
foons and mountebanks. This supplementary group included Beolco who,
not being a patrician, was unable to join.

Carnival—within whose temporal bounds youths suspended rules, questioned authority, and swept away the dead and useless—embodied a series of
rites termed *liminal* by anthropologist Victor Turner.[5] Liminal rites are ones
in which young people are segregated in order to examine the rules of the society. They are permitted some latitude of conduct, perhaps to smooth the
transition from unstructured to structured behavior. At the end of the period
of seclusion, they accept the norms of conduct and rejoin society. Thus, as
Turner has observed, youthful departure from the social structure functioned
as preparation for adult incorporation into it. Like members of college frater-
nities, Stocking Troupe members, while engaged in apparently frivolous activities, learned the ritualistic performances by which their class displayed
and retained its privileges. They also consolidated their positions in the nas-
cent power structure of their generation, forming bonds that would serve
them in the political career expected of adult patrician males.

Plot and Characters.   The *Pastoral*'s setting in the countryside near
Padua provides a meeting place for two antithetical groups of characters,
Tuscan-speaking Arcadian shepherds concerned with love, and Paduan-
speaking peasants worried about the everyday problems of life. A third
group, a Bergamasque-speaking doctor and his servant, mediates between

the two. The duality manifests itself in the play's two prologues, one in Paduan country dialect, delivered by a peasant, the other in literary Tuscan, delivered by an Arcadian shepherd.

The peasant Ruzante opens the first prologue by stumbling sleepily onto the stage and deciding to take a nap. He awakens suddenly, afraid that he has died in his sleep, and bites into a piece of bread to prove he is still alive. Satisfied, he realizes that he must have been dreaming.[6] He was in a paradise full of laughing girls, and one (Siringa) came along talking of Love, but she was crying. A besotted old man (Milesio) followed behind her and started to play a song. The girl runs away to the grange hall, leaving the old man despondent.

Another shepherd (Mopso) comes along, but the old man sends him away and kills himself. Returning, Mopso finds him and swoons. A third shepherd (Arpino) discovers the pair. At first he decides not to bury them, but when a fourth shepherd (Lacerto) convinces him that leaving them unburied would be dishonorable, Arpino is willing to try. Lacerto, however, deserts his companion after helping with only one of the bodies, claiming to be afraid of a wolf who inhabits the area. The disconsolate Arpino finally manages to enlist the aid of a local peasant (Ruzante) who, picking up Mopso, announces that he is still alive. Arpino fetches the doctor (Doctor Francesco), and Mopso is cured. Then, the narrator says, he saw them all run off and sacrifice a lamb. Recalling his own neglected duties to hunt birds for supper, he utters a swift farewell and rushes away.

The Tuscan prologue gives a very different version, noting Padua's reputation as "of all the liberal studies pupil and mother"[7] and home of Minerva and the Muses. More recently, however, the warlike Mars has been troubling the city. Minerva fled, but is preparing to return in glory. During her absence, the arts have continued to flourish like an untended garden, putting forth saplings and suckers. Original wits have been at work, seeking not fame but entertainment.[8] The declaration is followed by a brief outline of the plot.

To these summaries must be added most of the details about the peasant character. When Arpino asks his help, Ruzante explodes, accusing the shepherd of scaring away the bird that he has been tracking, and complaining that he has three mouths to feed plus his sister whose husband was killed by the Germans. The Arcadian promises him anything if he will help, but the peasant doesn't understand Tuscan. In frustration, the Arcadian cries out to the woodland god Pan. Here, at last, is a word Ruzante can understand, but in his dialect it means bread. Thinking that he has been offered some for his services, he steps smartly up to help and provides an offhand diagnosis: "He's not dead, but fallen in a faint / Just like Trivelun's two mares did" (*RT,* 63). He urges Arpino to get a doctor, but warns of their greed. After the Arcadian departs Ruzante kicks himself for not realizing that if he'd left the man for dead he could have taken his overcoat. But he consoles himself with a crafty plan to eat as much as he can of the shepherd's food; since his family knows nothing about it, he can then go home and eat again.

Arpino finds the doctor, who is sorry to hear that someone has died for unrequited love because as a medical student he learned that any woman's heart can be softened with money. Ruzante too seeks the doctor, for the father "who shat me into the world" (*RT,* 85) and makes him run around the countryside and into the city (Padua) on errands. The old man tripped and fell, but, to Ruzante's frustration, didn't break his head. The young peasant's soliloquy of anger melts into sweetness when his thoughts turn to his lovely Betia. But as he remembers the (perhaps successful) advances made to her by two neighbors, his ire is rekindled. Ruzante then encounters his buddy Zilio, who chides him for not pressing his advantage with Betia. The peasant admits his weakness, but promises to make up for it in the future.

Finding the doctor, Ruzante explains the problem and asks for something that will put his father out of his misery. When the medical man tells him to bring the father's urine (*l'orina*), Ruzante thinks he has asked for the cow Lorina in payment, and quickly protests that she was stolen by the Germans. She actually has been lent to some neighbors, as the audience eventually learns from a conversation that Ruzante has with Zilio on his way to get the specimen. Zilio asks if he can add his urine to the phial to obtain two diagnoses for the price of one. He will pay Ruzante, he promises solemnly, when he gets married (i.e., is paid a dowry).

Returning with the specimen, Ruzante is quizzed by the doctor about his father's symptoms. He does not respond to the questions, but delivers a tirade on the father's faults, especially how much he eats and how little he works. After a long argument full of mutual misunderstandings, Ruzante goes home to apply a poultice to his father's injury. He comes back rejoicing that the old man has died and left him "the mares and the cows and the pigs" and a field (*RT,* 131).

Ruzante runs to congratulate the doctor and offer him a present, finding him with the Arcadian characters who are preparing to celebrate the renewed health of the shepherd with an offering to Pan. He bids farewell to the audience:

> May Lady Saint Catherine
> bring you a backache.

> May Sir Saint Sebastian
> keep you from bread.
> May Sir Saint Footrubber
> keep you from health,
> And . . .
> I don't want to stand here yakking any more
> (*RT,* 141).

The young peasant chooses his partner, and the play closes with a dance.

Analysis. The *Pastoral* was closely linked to theatrical and literary conventions of its times, although it introduced a number of innovations. Like the plays of the pre-Rozzi of Siena, the *Pastoral* includes both Arcadian and peasant characters. The peasants in the Beolco play, however, are independent, rather than employed by the Arcadians, as in Sienese theater.[9] Literary critics have discerned a variety of references to learned literature in the Arcadian section of the *Pastoral*, especially Jacopo Sannazaro's *Arcadia,* Angelo Poliziano's *Favola d'Orfeo (Fable of Orpheus),* Boccaccio's *Ninfale fiesolano (Comedy of the Fiesolan Nymphs),* Petrarch's poetry, and echoes of Latin writers who influenced the Renaissance, such as Virgil. Beolco's references are seldom reverent, though. More often they ridicule the empty artificiality of written conventions divorced from reality.

The *Pastoral*'s mixture of different character types was a practice prevalent in Venetian spectacles.[10] The Bergamasque characters Doctor Francesco and his servant Bertuolo are rooted in various local theatrical traditions: the farce, buffooneries, aristocratic pageants, and macaronic literature (a satire of defective Latin learning). The peasant section of the play draws upon two local currents: the re-creation of the daily lives of the peasants, particularly the sufferings wrought by war, and the inclusion of individual peasant characters in aristocratic performances, as happened at the 1520 party. Aristocratic appreciation of rural life has been connected by Baratto with peasant support of Venice during the destructive Wars of Cambrai, widely perceived as an essential ingredient of Venetian success.

A deeper psychological factor seems also to have been at work. The battle of Agnadello in one swift stroke changed Venice from dominator to dominated. The prevalence of submissive figures, servants, and peasants in the painting and literature of Italy during the late fifteenth and early sixteenth centuries, when its city-states were enduring defeat at the hands both of other Europeans and of the Turks, points to a realization that, in the larger balance of power, Italian city-states' relations with European nation-states echoed those of peasants and servants with aristocrats.[11] Peasants symbolized both

the aristocrats' new status and the group within their own society that aristocrats could dominate to compensate themselves for the external loss. Such a
dynamic may partly explain why, in their new role as landlords, Venetian aristocrats tied the peasants to the soil and appropriated much of what they produced (an attitude whose regressiveness Baratto noted), though such choices
also, of course, produced clear economic benefits.

The question that critics face in interpreting the *Pastoral* is that of the
value assigned by the playwright to each of the three components (learned,
farcical, and peasant). While some see the play as catering to learned literary
modes and mocking country people,[12] Baratto sees Beolco as innovating
through the sympathetic realism with which he portrays the peasant world,
which dominates the piece. Ruzante is the character who both opens and
closes the comedy, and he is played by Beolco, who would become so well
known by that name that he would use it in legal documents. The struggle of
Ruzante and his companions to remain independent from city dominance
also indicates that the playwright prized them above Arcadians. Unfortunately, however, the world of city people has the power to victimize them.
"The essence of the character is therefore his 'interior' resistance to the external world."[13]

Resistance is achieved through the exploitation of Carnival license to question, before an audience, every form of authority: the father, the doctor, city
people, formal literature. His questioning, as Baratto has noted, makes
public their absurd inadequacy, provoking a laughter in Ruzante that both
challenges the aristocratic system and eases the pain of his impotence. Perhaps the most revealing episode is that of the burial of the two Arcadians
(scenes 8 to 9). When Arpino discovers the bodies, he is filled with chagrin,
fearing that if he buried them as suicides, he and they would lose the respect
of their companions.[14] He decides therefore to leave their bodies exposed,
and to carve a poem upon a nearby rock "to hide your infamy and dishonor"
(*RT,* 47). Arpino's reaction, apparently a reflection of humanists' postwar
concern for reputation, reveals that high-sounding Arcadian values are
empty formulas to be manipulated.

That pattern is repeated by Lacerto. Though believing in the dishonor of
exposure, he is not willing to exert much effort toward burial. After his hasty
departure, Arpino laments:

> Oh changeable and miserable world, I see
> every harsh vice reign over your entire expanse,
> and people offering any service for gold.

From the very moment the body is formed in infancy
those people don't care about the torments of friends
as long as they can pile up silver in their storeroom.

If you make yourself pitiful, they become hard.
That copper that through secrecy and violence they continue
    to steal from you
gives them so much false pride.

With phony ways and treacherous plots
first they flatter you and then they gnaw at you
because underneath they hide base cravings.

If you are reduced to poverty, they don't hear you,
but pretend not to know you, and walk on by;
in the end they delight in your every loss.

Then if by chance they are brought low,
they put honey on their evil tongues,
so that they hurt you more than a switch does a lamb.

I tell you, I'm not wrong because I've seen it proven
by this cruel shepherd, who was so anxious to show
that he was blinded by his sorrow for them

and now, fearing some dubious loss,
has gone on his way, and here, well out of my mind,
he leaves me. But that's how friends act (*RT,* 55).

The character who does help Arpino is, of course, Ruzante, a peasant used
to the mutual assistance upon which rural communities depend, and whose
compensation (both here and with the family to whom he has loaned Lorina)
comes in the form of bread, the necessary fuel for his long work days. It is
only later that he realizes that he acted against his own economic best interest
in missing the opportunity to claim the "dead" man's clothes, a response that
may be used to refute Giorgio Padoan's characterization of him as greedy.

As Baratto has noted, Ruzante lies only when he is under assault by a more
powerful character. He borrows a past truth (the cow being stolen by the Germans, a relic of the terrible devastation wrought by the war[15]) or a substan-
tive truth (he is responsible for feeding his relatives although technically he is
not the head of the family because his father is still alive) to protect himself. It
should be added that it is then too that he tries to give himself substance
through another oral act, overeating. This occurs, for example, when his honesty and his sympathy for Arpino result in a loss to him, and again in scene 18
when he is under pressure from the doctor, his father, and crafty Zilio.

Arpino's lie, on the other hand, is the premeditated construction of a façade to conceal the truth. He plans to manipulate the opinions of the Arcadians by suppressing the evidence of suicide (of which they disapprove) and emphasizing the shepherds' susceptibility to love (a tenet of the Arcadian code of which they do approve). It is, moreover, a lie that sacrifices the bodies of his friends to the beasts of carrion.

It is logical at this point to ask what drove Beolco to create and espouse an underdog character who fights to establish himself against the intrusive, self-serving control of family, learning, and aristocracy. A comparison of the circumstances of his life with the issues that he raises in his plays leads to the hypothesis that the character Ruzante is an expression of the playwright's anger with the circumstances of his own life, specifically his illegitimacy. As was mentioned above, illegitimacy deprived the individual of most means of controlling his life, delegating them to others, a fate shared by the peasant character invaded by a more powerful outside world.

The two characters who oppress Ruzante in the play bear some resemblance to Giovanni Francesco, responsible for Angelo's illegitimacy, as well as to the archetype of social authority that he represents, and that declares illegitimacy a problem. Doctor Francesco, with whom Ruzante engages in the most prolonged and hostile verbal battles, shares name and profession with the senior Beolco,[16] so intent as a youth on acquiring the Tuscan learning of the Arcadians. As will be shown below, the *Pastoral's* father who expects his son to run his business while he lives in semiretirement in the country also resembles Angelo's father. The number of mouths that Ruzante is responsible for feeding (three) is the number of Beolco's half-brothers.[17] The country names cited (Granze, Nogaroli, Prati del Peraro) are ones which may be found around Pernumia, as may the name Ruzante, a common surname in the region even today. Perhaps the parricide and inheritance that conclude the play are the products of Beolco's wishful thinking about his own life. Arpino's lament, however, seems a bitter realization of its more likely course, and of the dominant figures' exploitation of his vulnerability to enrich themselves.

The roots of Beolco's sensitivity to peasant problems are dual. His illegitimacy placed him in a social position analogous to theirs, and, in losing his mother, he had suffered personally from their helplessness. Of the three groups of characters, the one that wins his sympathy is that to which his putative mother most probably belonged, a figure whose absence from his life is echoed in the play. Probably of peasant origin, certainly a speaker of dialect, taken advantage of by Beolco's father, then apparently fired from her post, she is the person whose polemic is voiced in the *Pastoral*.

The playwright's anger and frustration seem to derive from the conflict between his ability to see the peasants' problems and the impossibility of his finding a solution within the existing social structure. He seems to have used the *Pastoral* to make the aristocratic members of his audience, landowners in the Paduan countryside and governors of the Venetian Republic, aware of the problems by making them live as peasants do. This, in fact, is the substance of his closing "prayer": he asks that the audience, like peasants, suffer from the hunger and illness that chronically threatened to rob the country people of their ability to work and thus endangered their lives.[18]

First Oration: Literary and Social Manifesto

Manuscripts, Date, and Performance. The *First Oration (Prima Oratione)* is one of the few Beolco plays whose date is relatively uncomplicated. One of the three manuscripts bears the statement that it was "recited to Cardinal Cornaro at the [Villa] Barco below Asolo in the Trevisan countryside."[19] The probable occasion for Beolco's speech was the 1521 entrance into Padua of Cardinal Marco Cornaro, named its bishop in 1517.

Cardinal Cornaro arrived at his see on the feast of the Assumption in mid August, and was feted in Padua for the next two weeks. He then retreated to the cooler, more relaxed atmosphere of the Villa Barco. Originally the country residence of former queen of Cyprus Caterina Cornaro, the villa then belonged to the Cardinal's father, Zorzi (Giorgio), who had attended the second of Beolco's 1520 performances in Venice. The Barco already enjoyed literary fame as the setting for the *Asolani* of Cardinal Bembo, a text whose discussion of amorous questions concluded with a strong affirmation of the spiritual advantages of Neoplatonic love. While there, the bishop was regaled by the *First Oration,* Beolco's version of the conventional welcome speech recited in Paduan dialect by a peasant figure, perhaps in the outdoor loggia that still stands. The audience may have included peasants from the area who gathered to hear the actor known for his ability to reproduce their speech.[20]

The preceding months had been successful ones in both personal and professional terms. On 2 January, Beolco and Alvarotto presented the sole play at an all-night party sponsored by the Company of the Farmers,[21] the first of numerous associations with that troupe. A few months later, Angelo's father had given him power of attorney, probably because he was then living in the country and wished to have someone look after his business in town.[22] Beolco's first recorded association with Alvise Cornaro, the wealthy landowner who would later become his patron, occurred on 20 April when he and

Marco Alvarotto acted as witnesses to a complex land transaction that Cornaro had undertaken for the Venetian patrician Bembo and Contarini families. The *First Oration*'s allusion to "my boss" is frequently taken to mean that the patronage relationship, which would become vital to Beolco in the future, had entered its initial stage.

Content. The orator explains to Cornaro that because he is a gentleman and does not go where he's not supposed to, he did not go to Padua to deliver his speech. The learned university men there would not have like it because city people make fun of country people. He has come instead to the Barco on behalf of the whole Paduan territory to explain his thoughts. They chose him as their speaker rather than those priests or grammarians because they like to keep their natural standing straight up and move their tongues in their own way, not the Florentine way.[23] He could speak Neapolitan (i.e. Florentine) if he wanted to, he assures the Cardinal, giving a garbled sample, but he doesn't want to, because he wants to keep his natural straight.

Padua's virtues are extolled in the following section. The poet Petrarch, although he was born in Florence, came to die in Paduan territory. The founder of the whole region was the Trojan hero Antenor, who came to the Pavan (Paduan countryside) to found Padua. "And our old ancestors wanted Padua to have a feminine name, so that she would always stay underneath the Pavan" (*RT,* 1187). The chief riches of the countryside are agricultural: birds, fruits, and grains grow there in profusion. Women—beautiful, hardworking, capable of carrying "three babies in a litter"—are its crowning glory.

Disparaging the inflated, humanistic image of Cornaro propounded in Padua, the peasant orator affirms that the Cornaro family is not Roman[24] but Venetian. Their name derives from the dogwood, a sound, hard, useful wood used in a number of farm implements. "Then, they make me almost crap from laughing, when they say that you are a great man. But don't they see you, the clap eat them? You're a little man, not a great man" (*RT,* 1195). The bishop also receives some advice on handling threats that would never have come from all the learned men whose speeches the peasant orator heard with his master: "it is better to live a coward than die a hero."

On the grounds that no one has seen Paradise,[25] the orator rejects the conventional etymology of "cardinal" as its hinge. His country friends define "cardinal" as a person who in this world lives the good life and then, when he dies, takes a hinge off the door of Paradise so he can get in anyway. He promises Cornaro that he has no interest in being a cardinal himself, and that he sees the two of them as equals, asking for assurances that Cornaro is not "one of those arrogant people who always want to be over everyone else and subjugate everyone" (*RT,* 1199). Urging him to continue on that path, the orator declares that the village assembly sent him to obtain just and necessary new laws, including the following.

People should be allowed to miss Mass on Sunday if they go hunting for pleasure rather than profit. Peasants should not be required to go hungry; they should be permitted to gather their crops in time of bad weather even if it is a church feast and to eat as much as they can. Priests should be either castrated or married so that they do not father children on the peasant women that their husbands then have the expense of raising. Finally, to reduce enmity between country and city, peasants should be allowed four spouses each. City men, who are already known for their love of peasant women, would flock to the country, and so would city women, so they could have four husbands. "And in this way, we will all be one and the same, and there will be no more envy and enmity, because we will all be one family" (*RT,* 1203). Every woman would bear children and everyone would have work to do.

The orator closes by assuring the cardinal that he is asking him this for the cardinal's own good. "Without me, what would you be? And we will all treat you as father, son, and brother, which we wouldn't do otherwise. Let's shake hands and promise me that in the future I can come and fetch the edict. God help you" (*RT,* 1205).

Analysis.   Having outlined his reasons for rejecting the old system of social authority in the *Pastoral,* Beolco chose the *First Oration* as the vehicle for proposing a new one. In this he heralded what Victor Turner has defined as one of the most significant shifts in the history of Western culture, that from liminal to liminoid. Industrialization introduced a number of changes during the late Middle Ages and the Renaissance that broke down the conservative, liminal cycle, promoting the development of a liminoid approach in which "the individual innovator, the unique person who dares and opts to create" is privileged, and the return to the rules is suspended. A typical result is that "supposedly 'entertainment' genres of industrial society are often *subversive.*"[26]

Addressing topics directly rather than in the more emblematic fashion of a play, the speech offers crucial evidence of the innovativeness of Beolco's views. The bolder statement of his polemic may have been the result of his recent success and, as Giovanni Calendoli has noted, of his association with Cornaro, who had proposed that Venice use the agricultural resources of the mainland to assure a political independence that would end damaging and unstable alliances with other states.[27] Additionally, Beolco seems to have gained a certain authoritativeness from his legal responsibilities for his retired father, visible in the firm way in which he issues the closing instructions to the bishop.

The change is manifested in a more open attack on formal culture. Jose Oliveira Barata has shown, for example, that the *First Oration* mocks in detail the clichéd humanistic welcome speech whose model had been followed faithfully by the university's public orator Marino Becichemo in official Paduan ceremonies.[28] As a result, according to Oliveira Barata, "the mask of pedantry fell, destroyed by laughter, empty formalism fell to make way for the recreation of the 'form' through the exaltation of a healthy, almost evangelical reality."[29] In this and in his other works, as Nino Borsellino observed, Beolco "makes use of pre-established formats subverting them from inside as a part of his faithfulness both as a man and as an artist to the world of the peasants."[30]

The precise nature of the philosophy that Beolco substitutes for empty rhetoric has been defined by Ronald Ferguson, who sees an alternative morality at work.[31] Contrary to Christian formulations, in which morality is concerned with meeting the needs of the spirit, Beolco's natural philosophy is an optimal version of the peasant world which defines the good as that which promotes physical life. Thus the laws Beolco proposes facilitate the gratification of bodily appetites, specifically those for food, sex, and the wholesome entertainment of the hunt.

The fervor characterizing the speech appears to have been inspired by the spiritual reform movement sweeping Europe at the time, as well as by Beolco's status as natural, or illegitimate, son. Beolco apparently became familiar with the movement's activities through the large numbers of foreign students in Padua and through Venetian acquaintances. For example, Marino Giustinian, a member of the Company of the Farmers with whom Beolco had performed that Carnival, had recently returned from a lengthy stay in London where his father was close to Thomas More, who introduced the senior Giustinian to Erasmus.

Beolco incorporates into the *First Oration* the tenets of both radical and moderate reform philosophies most likely to advance his proposals. Infused with the spirit of More's Utopia, his Paduan countryside is a kind of earthly paradise where the peasants live a natural life blessed by agricultural abundance. However, as in Utopia, their happiness is disturbed by the exploitation of outsiders, chiefly city people. To solve the problem, Beolco introduces a kind of radicalized Erasmian Folly that acts not as the leavening facilitating the rules, but as the fundamental rule itself. For example, like More, Beolco proposes that city people and country people mix; however, he turns to the iconoclastic Free Spirit movement for the solution of multiple spouses.[32] The concupiscence of clerics, criticized by More and Erasmus, elicits an approach from Beolco that surpasses even that of the latter philosopher: a choice between castration and marriage that again originates in the radical canon. The presentation of the *First Oration*'s radical manifesto at Villa Barco was significant for a number of reasons. Having been the site of Bembo's *Asolani* (a text and author embodying the profound split between expressed, idealizing beliefs and lived, self-indulgent practices that Beolco wished to defeat), the villa gave Beolco the opportunity to meet the enemy on his own ground, and even favored his position. Located outside cities and designed to provide intermittent escape from them, villas were among the first examples of architectural adaptation to liminoid values. From the onset of their popularity in Boccaccio's time, they separated work from play and served as loci for the leisured examination of social rules. Villas' increasing importance in the Veneto during the Renaissance, when they came more and more to serve as full-time residences for the wealthy, indicates a general social drift toward the liminoid, probably encouraged by the aristocracy's recent loss of power. It was a development upon which Beolco would soon attempt to capitalize in his Venetian performances.

Like the *Pastoral*, then, the *First Oration* provides evidence that Beolco closely observed the latest cultural trends to find material to adapt to his own purposes.[33] In reformulating it for his audience, he followed a brilliant two-phase persuasive strategy particularly suited to the oral medium. He first alluded to respected treatments of social problems to gain authority, then shrewdly liberalized their solutions to move his audience closer to his own views, adding punch with implied threats of angry peasant reactions. The strategy would prove fundamental to the next segment of his career.

Chapter Three
Ruzante Goes to Venice

The *Playful Letter:* Ruzante Farms the *Hortus Conclusus*

Manuscript, Performances, and Date. The commonly used title *Playful Letter* abbreviates "A Letter That Ruzante Writes to a Love of His," as the work is entitled in its only manuscript, the large miscellany discovered by Lovarini in the Marciana Library of Venice.[1]

After a quiet performance with the Company of the Farmers in 1521, Beolco grew more and more daring between 1522 and 1526.[2] On 3 March 1522, hosted by the Company of the Gardeners, he and Alvarotto put on what Sanudo disdainfully termed "a certain country-style comedy" at the home of the London Contarini. The "lord of the evening" was Gasparo Contarini, something of a wild man even in the context of the Stocking Troupes. During the Carnival of the next year, Beolco presented a play in the neighborhood of the Crosechieri monastery, which Sanudo ignored. When it was repeated in May at the Ducal Palace for the wedding of Antonio Grimani (grandson of the Doge), however, the diarist recalled the earlier staging and condemned the wedding performance as "a very ill-mannered thing to do in front of the Signoria [the city's top officials]." Beolco had apparently tried to expand Carnival license beyond its established boundaries of time and place, a boldness perhaps inspired by the success of Machiavelli's sexually and politically licentious *Mandragola* at the previous year's festivities.[3]

Two days after the wedding, the elderly Doge died. Shortly thereafter Andrea Gritti, aided by his fame as subjugator of Padua and by a family alliance with the extremely wealthy banker Alvise Pisani, was elected his successor. The autocratic new Doge was not well received by all, however. He and Pisani were the apparent targets of accusations that Venice would be transformed from a republic into a monarchy. And his predilection for the French, who exemplified centralized authority and often opposed the Emperor, provoked the resentment of many patricians.[4]

In 1524 Beolco performed with the Farmers, though not in a patrician home, perhaps because of the previous year's excesses. Instead, the men marched in procession around Venice, dressed as peasants and carrying hoes, shovels, rakes, and musical instruments. They made stops at the Ducal Palace to demonstrate their talent to the new Doge, and then at the Procuratia of Marco da Molin, a high-spirited member of the Immortals.

In 1523 Giovanni Francesco Beolco named his legitimate brother Giovanni Jacopo the agent for all his commercial dealings, presumably abandoning the power of attorney he had given Angelo two years earlier. Between 10 March 1524 and summer of the following year, the elder Beolco died, leaving his estate to his three legitimate sons, dowries of five hundred ducats to his two daughters, and twenty-five ducats to Angelo to be paid out in two yearly installments, each approximately equal to the annual pay of an infantryman, the army's lowest rank.[5]

The date of the *Playful Letter* is the subject of controversy because of the text's reference to protective measures taken against a flood. Lovarini, noting widespread astrological predictions for torrential rains and flooding in February of 1524, assigned the play to that year. However, he later seemed inclined to the date 1522. In a note to a second edition of the anonymous poem entitled *The Peasants' Alphabet* also containing references to the flood, he discussed the impact of prophecies published between 1522 and 1524. He also left among his papers a remark that a reference to the flood contained elsewhere in the Marciana manuscript might read 1522 rather than 1524 (as he had previously believed), a judgment confirmed independently by manuscript expert M. Cristofari.[6]

Ludovico Zorzi, stressing the *Playful Letter*'s similarities with Beolco's early works, assigned it a date of 1521–22, connecting it to the performances with the Gardeners and the Farmers. That chronology was rejected by Giorgio Padoan; returning to the question of the flood, he stated that he had found prognostications for 1524 only, not 1522. He disputed Cristofari's transcription of 1522, declaring that he read 1524, and postulated that the play's reference to German students would have been more appropriate in 1524, a period of Imperial alliance. Assigning the latter date to the *Letter,* Padoan noted its appropriateness to the Carnival procession of that year. He hypothesized that the Farmers could haves stopped at the home of Francesco Donà, greeted in the *Letter*'s closing, who had recently returned from Padua where he had been the Venetian magistrate. Zorzi rejected Padoan's chronology in an article written shortly before his death, supporting his views with evidence from Lovarini and A. Luzio.[7]

Zorzi's position is strengthened by recent research demonstrating that 1522 also figured in the prophecies. Luca Gaurico, an astrologer who enjoyed the patronage of Marino Grimani (grandson of the Doge), repeatedly predicted that floods would begin in September of that year.[8] In Germany,

1522 was paired with 1524 in the prophecies of doom; in the earlier year, it was predicted, "the peasants will form an association against the nobility" and the old Imperial order will fall and be replaced by a new one.[9] Extremely heavy rainfall and flooding occurring in February of 1522 may have seemed a warning of what would follow, prompting the precautions spoofed in Beolco's joking proposal to build risers on top of the Belltower of St. Mark. A second clue as to the play's date is provided by the list of states included in Ruzante's denunciation of people who adopt foreign styles. It corresponds to those grouped around the Emperor in late 1521 and early 1522: Florence, Hungary, and Naples. The criticism makes sense in 1522, when Venice was allied with the French and opposed to the Emperor, a situation that would reverse itself by 1524. The reference to German students could be a typical example of Beolchian sarcasm, as might the greeting to Donà, in 1522 a candidate for the magistracy of Padua.

Given Beolco's more frequent association with the Imperial faction, his favoring of Venice's anti-Imperial affiliation is surprising, and may have been predicated upon a hope of patronage by the ducal Grimani family. The Farmers, with whom Beolco had performed in 1521, were the Stocking Troupe of the Doge's grandson, Marco. Headstrong enough to engage in armed combat with his uncle over who would run the Doge's household, Marco seems to have liked the playwright's flamboyant style: it was with the Farmers that Beolco entertained at the 1523 wedding.[10]

The question of a 1522 performance is problematic. As Beolco's was the sole play at the performance recorded by Sanudo for that year, the text was probably not the *Playful Letter,* which is only two pages long. As in 1523, however, Sanudo may have chosen to omit another Beolco performance. Cherea, a noted classical actor with whom Beolco later performed, staged a tragedy in the Ducal Palace on 2 February 1522 at the behest of Marco Grimani. Guest of honor was the bishop of Ivrea, then a student in Padua. The *Letter* may have been performed then as an intermezzo, the type of between-act entertainment to which its length suited it.

A date of 1522, one which the present author finds likely, does not exclude the possibility that the monologue was presented again in 1524, perhaps with modifications.

   Content.   Despite being called a letter, the text is a performance piece of the kind termed a *sprolico,* as Zorzi noted. Such texts, especially the *Letters* of Beolco's follower Andrea Calmo, would frequently serve as the bases for theatrical performances later in the century. Giorgio Padoan has pointed out that the *Playful Letter* follows the three-part structure of the epistolary genre: preamble, subject, and petition.[11]

The play, a monologue, is delivered by a peasant, who opens with Beolco's oft-stated criticism of learned show-offs. Even when they write someone a letter, "they have to talk in Tuscan like people do in Florenceland, and in Spanish, and in the Neapollution way, and like the Hungry-uns, and like they want to be sold like soldiers" (*RT,* 1247). Imitating pompous speech, the soliloquist notes that people who use that sort of language do so to make themselves seem more important, but succeed only in getting themselves laughed at by everyone, including himself.

Good, natural Paduan is the only language for him. Why, people come from all around to learn Paduan, even the sons of German gentlemen who go so far as to become servants to do so. But the peasant is more interested in another matter, that of the farm of the woman he is addressing, which she said she would give him the other day, when he was in her room. He has a proposal for her. Since the time of pruning the vines is swiftly approaching, he will bring his tools and she can hire him by the day. She will be happy with his work since his shovel digs deep, and its shaft stays firmly in place. If he works her farm for a season, it will produce more and better and more willingly than if anyone else had touched it.

The peasant concludes by saying that he has heard a lot of weeping and wailing about a flood that is supposed to come, and asks if she will get some of her friends to build him a riser on top of the Belltower of St. Mark (the tallest building in the region). At least that way he'll be among the last to die. He advises her to make sure that she, too, is in a safe spot, concluding "in the meanwhile, I'll make a bow to you and to sir Francesco Donà" (*RT,* 1248).

Analysis. Zorzi saw the *Playful Letter* as a variation on the tradition of the *hortus conclusus,* the garden of chaste, refined delights with which the aristocracy separated itself from the common people. Firmly rejecting Lovarini's romantic fancy that the *Letter* was a private missive of Beolco's to an enamoured aristocrat, Zorzi viewed it as a performance piece that extended the metaphor of the garden, emblem of two of the Stocking Troupes with which Beolco entertained. It allowed him to address to a hypothetical beloved the kind of double entendres that he could not utter personally. Zorzi's interpretation was substantially followed by Padoan.

A richer understanding comes from Baratto's insight that Beolco's works aim to transform aristocrats into peasants. The playwright's efforts to impose his social views upon his audiences by dominating them are not to be neglected here. Beolco breaks into the closed space of the aristocratic garden and penetrates its soil, becoming its master and father of its descent line. This and his condescending reference to the inability of another to produce the same abundant harvest recall the plot of Machiavelli's *Mandragola.* There, an impotent elderly Florentine (Nicia) desires a child so badly that he schemes to have his wife impregnated by another man, who, he believes, will then be killed by a potion. Nicia's impulse is consistent with the patriciate's intense concern with producing a descent line to inherit its wealth and privileges. Indeed, some have seen Nicia as symbolizing Piero Soderini, the leader of the ill-starred Florentine Republic. There is, however, an important difference between Machiavelli and Beolco. While Nicia's child in any case remains the offspring of the patriciate because his substitute is the aristocratic Callimaco, in Beolco's play it is a peasant who generates the descent line.

On 13 February 1522 the *Mandragola* was staged in Venice for the first time by Cherea. Resonances of it in the *Playful Letter* imply that Beolco was familiar with Machiavelli's comedy and appropriated some of its themes. If the hypothesis of a 2 February 1522 performance of the *Playful Letter* is correct, Beolco, apparently induced by an intense need to fuel his polemic and to remain at the forefront of cultural trends, scooped two of his most acclaimed rivals shortly before opening night.

The *Betia:* The Peasant World Comes to Life

Performances. The daring which Beolco had demonstrated in 1523 at the Ducal Palace wedding reasserted itself during Carnival of 1525 at a rehearsal sponsored by the Company of the Triumphants and managed by ("di la qual é autor") Zuan (Giovanni) Manenti. It was attended by so many Senators and members of the Council of Ten that neither body could meet. Also present were several young Procurators of St. Mark, including Marco da Molin and Marco Grimani. The centerpiece of the show was a triple comedy staged by Manenti. "Then, Ruzante and Menato, Paduans [acting] as peasants, did a comedy in the country style and [it was] all lascivious and [full of] very dirty words, so much so that it was criticized by all, and there was much hue and cry about it. There were almost sixty women in [Carnival] mask on the risers, the young ones with their heads covered, that were horrified at what was said in their name. The whole conclusion was about screwing and cuckolding their husbands. . . . And at the conclusion of the rehearsal of the aforementioned comedy all expressed outrage, not at the Troupe members, who spent . . . ducats, but at the promoter [*autor*], and it was money earned [or: won] a year ago at the lottery."[12]

On opening night (February 13), Sanudo reports that "they did not have a performance of the dirty comedy, done [*fato*] for [*per*] the oil [or: Olio] guy for which he had fifty ducats but the one by Ruzante in the country style." On the basis of the passage, Padoan has questioned Beolco's authorship of the "dirty play," concluding that it was written by the figure he identifies as "that [guy] from the Oglio River [area]," possibly the actor who played the doctor in the *Pastoral*. The ambiguity does not seem to resolve itself so easily, however, because it involves the meanings of the words *fato* and *per*. The first is the past participle of one of the most general verbs in the language, translating frequently "made" or "done," but also functioning as a general verb substitute. The most obvious reading for the second is "for." In the 13 February passage, thus, Sanudo seems to have been indicating that "quel da l'oio" (Manenti, as he has been identified by most other scholars), the organizer for whom the evening's entertainment was executed, had chosen the dirty play (rather than writing it).

Manenti arrived in Venice at the same time as Machiavelli's *Mandragola*. He was sufficiently familiar both with the Florentine political theorist and with theatrical productions to write Machiavelli in 1526 urging him to send a play for a May performance. Manenti also conducted lotteries for the Venetian state. If he is "quel da l'oio," he perhaps first supervised the Triumphants' lottery win, then had fifty ducats of it paid over to himself as a fee for organizing the 1525 party, perhaps inspired by Marco Antonio Contarini of the Eterni who, when he won a suspiciously large lottery prize in 1524, feasted his troupe.[13] Manenti, who did not enjoy permanent employment as lottery manager but was hired on an ad hoc basis, may have attempted to use the 1525 play to ingratiate himself with the nobility who appointed him to his post. An aficionado of Machiavelli's daring plays, he may have urged Beolco to stage the "dirty comedy." When Manenti, whom Bibbiena had cited in the *Calandria* as a paradigm of foolishness, turned out to have made a mistake, another play of Beolco's was substituted.

A final possible explanation of a passage that, at least in some readings, would seem to reverse the identification of the two plays given in the rehearsal passage is that Sanudo confused them. Though one is reluctant to have recourse to such a solution, Sanudo did make similar errors.[14]

By the summer of 1525, Beolco had apparently moved from his father's home to that of Alvise Cornaro.[15] It is possible that Angelo's widowed stepmother, coping with five children and diminished financial resources, pressed him to leave. During this period, Cornaro frequently called upon his "familiaris" (servant) to witness documents for him. On 15 December 1525 Alvarotto lent a hand as well. The date is important, as Sambin has noted, because it occurs between two of the pair's particularly problematic performances, and may indicate that they were planning what was to come.

On 7 February 1526 a banquet was held on the Giudecca, a large island that encircles part of Venice, at the palace of the Trevisan family.[16] Three comedies were again presented, one by Cherea, a country-style one by Ruzante and Menato, and the last by Cimador. The guests included the Papal legate and ambassadors from the Holy Roman Empire, France, England, and Austria. Their retinues caused considerable disturbance at table; one Spaniard even threw a wine pitcher at a Venetian patrician. But the greatest shock came when a plucked and crestless rooster popped out of a pastry and careened around the table. Sanudo complained that the episode was ill-advised because of the presence of the French ambassadors (with whom some in the Venetian government were then negotiating an alliance opposed by many other patricians) and reported that it caused widespread grumbling. He particularly notes that four young procurators attended, including Marco and Vetor Grimani and Marco da Molin. The latter's efforts to disperse the crowd were resisted by many guests, who wanted to stay for Beolco's play. There is no record of what role Beolco may have played in the prank, but it is difficult to imagine him uninvolved.

As Lovarini noted, the hapless bird symbolized Francis I, king of France (in Italian, *gallo* means both "rooster" and "Gaul"). Captured the year before at the battle of Pavia by the king of Spain (Charles V, also Holy Roman Emperor), Francis was then being forced to accede to humiliating demands to obtain his release. A number of powerful Venetian patricians who had followed Beolco's recent boisterous performances (Luca Tron, Lorenzo Loredan, Jacomo Soranzo, Andrea Giustinian, Andrea Gusoni, Marco Molin) would soon absent themselves from the ceremony marking the third anniversary of Gritti's dogeship, near the time when the French alliance was concluded.[17] Those involved in the rooster episode, apparently including Beolco, seem to have shared sentiments in favor of the Emperor and against Gritti and France. A sense of Beolco's political affiliation may be gained by contrasting him with another actor, the buffoon Zuan Polo (Cimador's father) who had entertained with Beolco the year before. The same night as the rooster episode, Zuan Polo was playing the part of a doctor in a stately Ducal Palace procession, possibly deeming it wiser to show his allegiance to the doge.

The subsequent absence of Beolco's name from Sanudo's *Diaries* led Lovarini to hypothesize that he gave no further performances in Venice. That conclusion is supported by the declaration of Giandomenico Maganza, a follower of Beolco, that Padua would not have been audience to his late plays without Cornaro.[18] There are no records of Beolco's being formally sent into exile, but the Venetian system requiring government permission for entertainment made one unnecessary. The Council of Ten could simply have denied any requests involving him, or informed him by word of mouth that he was no longer welcome.

The turbulence visible in Beolco's performances also characterized his personal life. Perhaps remembering his uncle's lost legacy, he petitioned his stepmother and brothers for life-long maintenance from his father's estate, threatening to sue if he did not receive it. On 26 April 1526 a compromise was struck that allowed him a severance sum of one hundred ducats, sufficient to cover minimal expenses excluding rent for about eight years. Angelo was to receive twenty ducats immediately in cash, and collect the remaining eighty from rents on family property in Padua and Arquà, a town in the nearby Euganian hills.

A month later, Angelo squandered seventy ducats on an expensive horse bought from Giovanni Cornaro, a sum with which, as Sambin notes, he could have bought eight fields. Unable to pay, he signed his inheritance over to Alvise Cornaro, who covered the debt, reimbursing himself through the collection of the Beolco rents. Alvise Cornaro's gesture may have been intended to enhance his relationship with Giovanni Cornaro more than that with Angelo. Alvise wanted his daughter to marry Giovanni, an authentic Venetian patrician, to restore his descent line to an aristocratic status apparently lost by his ancestors, a goal he achieved eleven years later. By February 1527 Angelo had spent fifty ducats on another horse. Again unable to pay, he induced his in-laws to pawn their household valuables to meet the demands of the seller. Alvise Cornaro intervened a second time and retrieved the goods, though by giving the in-laws a loan rather than simply redeeming the items. Their promissory note is the first known evidence of Angelo's marriage, possibly contracted for its financial benefits.[19]

Manuscripts and Date. The *Betia* exists in two manuscripts, both discovered by Emilio Lovarini. An incomplete version is included in the Marciana miscellany, while a complete version exists in Venice's Correr Museum.[20] Because of the Marciana manuscript's large number of references to events occurring between 1510 and 1516, Lovarini at first assumed that the *Betia* dated to that period. He later discovered the Correr text, whose lack of polish induced him to believe it the earlier version. Its reference to coins called *mocenighe*, minted in 1524 by Doge Andrea Gritti for the first time in many years, caused Lovarini to revise the date to 1524. Lovarini identified the small, decorative Correr manuscript as a wedding gift to Antonio Grimani and his bride, commemorating the 1523 Ducal Palace performance, although the reference to the coins indicated to him that it had been given later. He also identified the *Betia* as the most likely candidate for the scandalous 1525 play. Lovarini's interpretations were accepted by Zorzi, who affirmed that the manuscripts represented respectively the texts performed at the Grimani wedding and the 1525 Carnival rehearsal.

Padoan rejected the views of both scholars on the grounds that the Grimani would have been insulted by the criticism of the previous doge implicit in the reference to Gritti's *mocenighe*. He agreed that the play was composed between late 1524 and mid 1525 and that the Correr manuscript contained the earlier version, but argued that the manuscripts date to the period 1526–27 and that the corrections evident in the second version demonstrate an interest in literary refinement belying Beolco's antiestablishment stance.[21]

Further research shows that the reference to *mocenighe* may point to Lovarini's original date. According to historian Antonio Bonardi, Paduan rebels insulted the Venetians during the War of Cambrai by saying that *mocenighi* stank of wine, a reference to monetary shortages that forced the Republic to scavenge table silver as material for coins.[22] Moreover, the *Betia*'s length, more than twice that of any other Beolco play, may have been due to the abundance of leisure time produced by the slowing of university life during the war. Further support for an early date is found in the fact that the events of the war years comprise the bulk of those mentioned in the play; later material is added in unassimilated blocks. The play's *congedo* (farewell speech; *RT,* 509) provides a good example. Its first half refers to recent wars and to Rome, Florence, and Urbino. The choice of the three cities is not casual; they were united under Medici rule from 1516 to 1519 through the tenacious efforts of Pope Leo X, a campaign that would have been particularly familiar to Beolco because the Pope's personal physician, Anton Francesco de' Dottori, was an executor of Giovanni Francesco Beolco's will. The second half contains a paraphrase of Boccaccio's authorial defense (discussed below) which probably dates to the early 1520s.

While thus endorsing the hypothesis of an early date for the original composition of the play, the present writer agrees with the traditional opinion that the Correr manuscript is linked with the Grimani wedding. The Marciana manuscript's single Paduan prologue indicates that it is a version undertaken after 1526 in Padua, possibly as an update of the original Paduan version.

Plot and Characters

The play, untitled in the manuscripts, has been given the name of the principal female character, apparently a variation on Beta (the common diminutive of Elizabeth). The added *i* lends intensity and recalls the term for a defective woman, *bettagna*. As with Balzac's *La Cousine Bette,* one suspects that the name was chosen for its animal overtones (*bestia* means "animal"), in this case cunning mixed with denseness, and concern for material pleasures over all else. An additional association may be with *betola* or tavern, one of the character's favorite haunts.[23]

The play is preceded by two prologues delivered by a peasant speaker, one for performances in Venice (found in the Correr manuscript only) and one for Paduan performances (found in both manuscripts). As Zorzi observed, the Paduan prologue, in which the author expresses his authentic sentiments, is the original one. The shorter prologue praising Venice was probably added when Beolco was invited to perform there. Both begin by declaring, "The natural between men and women is the most beautiful thing there could be," and point out the vitality of animals in the countryside (*RT,* 149, 153), a linking of human and animal (re)productivity echoing that of the *Playful Letter.* Both prologues then criticize pastoral literature and the linguistic pretentiousness of its writers, who want to call sheepherders shepherds and talk like Florentines. The *prologista,* on the other hand, is proud of having been born in Padua and wouldn't change his tongue for two hundred Florentine ones.

The admiration expressed in the Venetian prologue, rather than exalting the city, serves as a vehicle for what Salvatore Di Maria has called "blame-by-praise irony."[24] Venice is extolled as a place where nothing grows but anything can be found (perhaps an accusation that she appropriates the best from everywhere else). Venetian women are compared to the Virgin Mary, praise that is undermined by the further observation that in Venice one can even go to bed in a boat (the locus of many Venetian assignations). According to the *prologista,* "the whole reversal world" (both "universal" and "upside down" or perverted) runs to Venice, and then is unable to leave because of the respect for laws that characterizes the city. Perhaps more than one person in the audience was reminded by this of the arrest and confinement to Venice of the Paduan rebels of 1509, many of whom continued to be involved in legal proceedings until 1517 and were again brought to Venice in the troubled years between 1523 and 1530.[25]

The *prologista* lauds Venetian courage against the enemy, especially her valor against the Turks (leaving unstated her loss of major battles to them in the previous two generations) and in standing against the four greatest powers in the world. Venetian doges are praised for the coins they mint, among them *mocenighe.* The orator thanks God that he was born a man and not a woman, Italian and not French or German, and under the government of Venice and not another (possibly a snide allusion to mainland youths born under Imperial domination during the Cambrai period) because if people who are born under the Republic have material goods or a woman, they don't have to be afraid of having them taken away (perhaps sarcastic, as inhabitants of Venice's mainland dominion suffered depredations from both armies). He concludes, "And therefore I pray all the men and women saints that they grant us the favor that all the babies that *will be born or that have been born in these tribulations* will become paladins like Roland in war, and Aristotles and philosophers in the study of letters" (*RT,* 151; emphasis added).

The aspects of Padua that call forth praise are, above all, the people. The peasants in particular are singled out for their generosity in allowing anyone to stay in their houses and in sharing their bread (perhaps an ironic allusion to the billeting of Venetian troops with peasants and the plundering of the countryside by both sides). Padua's glories originated with her founding by Antenor of Troy (only slightly tarnished by the knowledge that *troia* is slang for a prostitute). The scholars at her university are so illustrious that they attracted Petrarch to the city so that he, who regretted not having been born there, could die there (a primal boast of the city's ability to kill Beolco's literary enemy).

The play itself opens with the lament of Zilio, who curses love for having shot an arrow into his stomach and not having yet touched his beloved. His friend Nale comforts him with the assurance that love is natural. He opines that although we all must experience love at least once because it is in love that our freedom is taken away, love's pain is remedied when its desire is attained. Two other friends (Bazarelo and Uncle Jerks[26]) arrive, turning the discussion into a debate. Bazarelo finds the current vogue for love a waste of time and recommends going to work instead. Zilio asserts that Love is a god, but Bazarelo retorts that it's all in your mind; no one has seen the God of Love.

Uncle Jerks, disciple of the greatest scholar in the Pavan (probably Bembo)—a greatness describing his appetite and girth as much as his learning—takes Zilio's side, confirming that Love is a god who makes things go against nature and reason. Frustrated at his inability to rebut Bazarelo's retort that love must be a devil because he hurts his servants, the dim-witted Jerks explodes. He beats Bazarelo, who finally admits that his reason for not believing in love is that he can't afford it. Jerks upbraids him for failing to realize that the purpose of love is marriage and children. Bazarelo replies that he is uninterested in marriage because a beautiful wife will cuckold you, and children cost too much and cause too much worry.

In act 2, attention returns to Zilio's problems: he is willing to get married but his beloved is not. The probable reason, he admits, is his lack of money, that substance that "makes crazies look learned and knowledgeable" (*RT,* 247). Nale's account of how he won his wife by spending lavishly at local fairs and impressing her with his dancing and singing skills depresses Zilio, an impoverished day laborer. As if on cue, Betia appears and is courted by Zilio, whom she briskly rejects. Nale, marveling at his friend's ineptitude, resolves to get her to run away with Zilio, so that he can then intervene and claim her for himself. When in act 3 he asks Betia why she doesn't like Zilio, she replies that he has to work too hard during the day to work hard enough at night. She accepts Nale's offer to resolve the problem by becoming her second husband. The three elope to avoid the censure of Betia's mother Menega, who later learns of their flight from a neighbor boy. On the road, Nale stops the trio to arrange the sharing of the bride. When Zilio realizes he is serious, he scolds his friend for his lack of conscience. The pause lasts long enough for Menega to arrive and drag her daughter back home, berating her for taking a mountain of household goods, though the daughter insists that she earned them. Menega also excoriates her daughter for her sexual appetite, but Betia slyly reminds Menega of her own premarital adventures.

Zilio and Nale reconcile in act 4 and plan the abduction of Betia. They are interrupted by Taçio, the local tavern owner and civil authority. He uses the threat of banishment to calm them down so they can tell him what happened. To Menega's laments that she wanted Betia to marry better, he replies that since the daughter caused the problem, she should marry Zilio as her penance. Discussing the plans for the wedding, the women begin to quarrel. Menega criticizes the groom, recalling the poverty that forced him to go to the bishop's relief for food during the famine year. The girl is brought to her senses, blames Love for her foolishness, and begs forgiveness.

Betia and Zilio's wedding ceremony opens act 5, with Taçio officiating and giving the scriptural, legal, and learned justifications for marriage: to increase and multiply. Menega responds by praising the sexual prodigality of her daughter. Afterwards, Nale reasserts his claim on Betia, enraging Zilio. He stabs Nale, who falls to the ground; Nale's wife Tamia rushes on stage and utters a moving lament. Her husband, who has not died, decides to have some fun and comes back disguised as a ghost to haunt her. She asks him a number of practical questions about hell, such as whether people feel pain when they die, and how souls can descend if they are smoke (which rises). Nale, caught off guard by such sophistication, fumbles through makeshift answers. They then discuss famous Venetian and Paduan residents of hell and their punishments.

Finally Tamia gets bored and announces to her husband that she is planning to remarry. When her suitor Meneghello arrives, Nale decides to put an end to the joke and reappears as himself. After a brief quarrel they make up, Tamia claiming that she wasn't really planning to remarry. Nale confides to the audience that he must accept her lie since he started the whole escapade.

He even asks Zilio's pardon for his actions, which he attributes to the devil. Explaining that Nale's only mistake was not making a contribution of his own, Zilio proposes that the two couples join together and make four contented people.[27] Meneghello, who skulks back on stage after they leave, vows that the contented will be five.

Analysis.   From a critical perspective, the most important characteristic of the *Betia*, as Grabher and Baratto have noted, is that it is the first play in which the author fully realizes an alternative society, rather than railing against the old one.[28] In the text and the performances of the play (as in the *First Oration*), Beolco pioneers a liminoid approach,[29] using the liminal as his point of departure. He chooses a peasant genre, the *mariazo* or marriage play, as the vehicle for his ideas.[30] He flaunts his connection with Padua, a city whose Trojan tradition, as he noted in the *First Oration,* places it outside the mainstream myth of Roman origin (of vital importance to Renaissance humanism), and whose connection with the university and location away from the capital also confer liminal status. The majority of Beolco's performances took place on the outskirts of Venice: Ca' Foscari, Crosechieri, Ca' Contarini da Londra, Ca' Arian at Angelo Raffaello, Ca' Trevisan on the Giudecca. His plays about a peasant world outside the normal experience of the audience were presented principally at Carnival, whose specific temporal bounds and license in sexual conduct and political criticism mark it as the liminal season par excellence. Beolco's Venetian companions were the members of the Stocking Troupes, groups whose liminal function has been demonstrated above. In the Venetian prologue of the *Betia,* Beolco praises the inhabitants for their use of boats, which, like other vehicles, are liminal structures in that they suspend the fixed identity linked to a specific place and group. Before the motor, they were perhaps the most so, as is recognized by the widespread use of sailor suits as clothing for children, the protagonists of liminality.

Beolco, who may have originally hoped to complete the liminal cycle by achieving social adulthood (as the *Pastoral* indicates) was stalled in the examining phase by his father's failure to legitimize him.[31] At the same time, he found himself in constant contact with aristocratic youths whose fathers' deaths would produce very different results, the transferring of control over the Republic of Venice to them. A good example is the case of Marco da Molin. Despite his arrest at a very young age for questionable activities in a convent, Molin began climbing the Venetian political ladder early in life, frequently obtaining offices through large money offerings. His father, a procurator of St. Mark, died in 1522. Marco, who had not yet reached the age of majority and thus should have been ineligible, hastily offered the enormous sum of fifteen thousand ducats to acquire the office for himself, and with equal haste married a wealthy bride whose dowry would provide it.[32]

Further blockage to Beolco's societal adulthood was created by a change in Venetian leadership form the empathetic Grimani to Andrea Gritti, whose belief in autocratic government was reified in the reconquest of Padua.[33] Gritti's political agenda privileged centralized, exclusive control, both in government and in cultural activities, where he strove to impose uniform Roman images of grandeur and to abolish less dignified folk art, particularly in Carnival festivities. During his dogeship, Venice moved away from its alliance with the rather loosely organized Holy Roman Empire and formed the League of Cognac with France, whose royalty provided a model of centralized power.

Apparently in response to such personal and political pressures, Beolco attempted to eliminate exclusion by creating a new, liminoid system of social values set in a peasant world of shared responsibilities and rewards. For the *Betia,* he thus chose the unstructured *mariazo,* using a tumultuously rendered rural dialect located at the opposite end of the spectrum from the humanists' rigidly structured Latin sentences,[34] whose predictable rhythms paralleled their model of an ordered society under their control. The *Betia*'s hero is a day laborer, the measure of whose poverty is its threat to his formation of the most elemental of human societies, marriage, and who mentions neither parental home nor family (their absence, however, is also a liberation from the primal form of patriarchy). Through his plays, Beolco attempted to impose an acceptance of liminoid social values upon the Venetian ruling class, an effort symbolized by the transferal of his 1523 Carnival Crosechieri performance from a peripheral location in both time and place to the seat of Venice's government.

The *Betia*'s opening sally employs one of the most fundamental forms of rebellion, the violation of sexual taboos. It turns the playful sexual puns characteristic of Renaissance comic prologues into a serious program of reform that not only legitimates Beolco's peasant but places him at the center of the order of things. Profanity, whose power "to (re)create this society, through a sudden disruption" has been recognized by many scholars including Luigi Monga and Mikhail Bakhtin,[35] continues to challenge authority throughout the play.

The expansion of liminal structures into liminoid ones also characterizes Beolco's use of authorizing texts. The debate about love is filled with references to Bembo's *Asolani,* the central text in that important contemporary issue and liminal in its examination of the definition of love in a pleasant rural retreat.[36] At every point Beolco pushes his subject farther than

Bembo, his ideological rival. Bembo describes an ideal world that he says does not exist;[37] Beolco describes the same world point for point, but it is the Paduan countryside (*RT,* 152–54). Bembo stresses the spiritual advantages of love; Beolco insists that it makes you do things against nature and reason. Even Bembo's physical presence is mocked in the *Betia,* especially the effect of his hearty eating upon the nether parts of his anatomy. Beolco's particular zeal in refuting Bembo may have stemmed from a sense of threat. Bembo moved to Padua in 1522; during that year he took religious orders and his Neoplatonic *Asolani* was reprinted. The following year, his first illegitimate child was born.

Thomas More's *Utopia* (as Charles Fantazzi noted, Utopia is the antithesis of the pastoral) and Erasmus's *Praise of Folly* also contribute material to the debate in the *Betia,* but again as the starting point for liminoid developments. Like Erasmus, Beolco affirms that animals and plants in the country are more alive than their counterparts in the city.[38] The entire play seconds illegitimately begotten *Folly*'s jovial disdain of learned idiocy in its characters' simple lives based on natural inclinations. Beolco's conclusion, however, unlike the Dutch scholar's, does not affirm religious faith as the antidote to the world's absurdities, but a social collective that rejects Christian sexual morality. Moreover, Beolco's characters, breaking for dinner between act 1 and act 2 like those of More's *Utopia* between book 1 and book 2, return praising the wine and food before resuming a discussion far less sober than that of the English characters.

In short, Beolco rejects the values of the Western tradition that divide people into high and low. Instead, he favors less exalted, more realistic norms that unite all living beings in a recognition of mutual rights and obligations. Such an attitude, by lessening the privileges of some, may provoke reprisals, as Beolco acknowledges in the *Betia,* whose characters are preoccupied with threats that society will use banishment and hanging to force them to conform to traditional codes of conduct. For example, when Bazarelo, who has hinted that he satisfies his sexual needs with his mares, reaches the point of rejecting procreation, Nale prophesies that he will one day dangle at the end of a hangman's noose. Bazarelo retorts that it is a proud family tradition that he embraces.

The structure of the wedding plot reifies Beolco's move toward a liminoid model. The independence that Betia gains from earning her own money and from her mother's failure to fulfill the parental duty to marry her permits Betia to assume control of her own life. She enlarges the peasant custom of premarital affairs, which her mother had enjoyed, into permanent change by taking two husbands. The elopement dispenses with the ceremony authorizing marriage and with the need for parental consent. Social rules are temporarily enforced by Taçio, but his subsequent injunction to increase and multiply reopens the possibility of change. For, while it is biblical, it is also rooted in the peasant ethic of enhancing life, and motivates a number of unbiblical peasant sexual practices.[39] In the play, in fact, it leads to irregular conduct, such as Menega's praise of Betia's premarital appetite, and the renewal of Nale's attempts to share the bride.

The "hell" that Nale creates is his permanent stopping place, not a waystation, like Dante's Inferno, where punishments frighten the sinner onto the road to heaven. Having removed himself from the framework of Christian salvation, Nale goes beyond even the reaches of peasant white magic (indicated when he says "You cannot carry / a fennel stalk" [*RT*, 459]) to a place where society is restructured for all eternity. The sinner wades through a sea of offal upon which floats a boatload of strumpets, whose resemblance to Sebastian Brant's recently published *Ship of Fools* has been noted by Franco Fido.[40] The peasants, however, at least have the satisfaction of torturing the soldiers, damned for the destruction they wrought upon country people.

As before, the group is temporarily pulled back within the bounds of normal behavior, this time because Tamia's desire to remarry prompts Nale to return from hell. However, it only provides the opportunity for Zilio, originally the enforcer of conventional morality, to initiate the final conversion to a liminoid system of open marriage based on a potentially limitless exchange system. Even this reform, which simply expands canonical marriage, is pushed farther by Meneghello's resolve to join the group despite his inability, as a bachelor, to contribute. His is a declaration that each individual has an absolute right to certain basic happinesses regardless of circumstances. Thus the play achieves one of the fundamental characteristics of the liminoid, that individuals participate by their own choice and empower themselves to change rules.

Such an analysis is confirmed by the *congedo*, where Beolco seems to quote Boccaccio's defense of the *Decameron* against charges of obscenity, although actually extrapolating from it to very different effect. The jovial medieval novelist excused his book by saying that even the Scriptures contain images capable of reminding people of anatomical functions, and mollifying his readers by asking them to skip objectionable parts. The Renaissance playwright, on the contrary, confronts his audience with the fact that, despite their protestations of innocence, they all know how babies get born. He warns them that when natural things are heard even from the pulpits of preachers, people must listen to them.

The vehemence of Beolco's protest indicates that he was uninclined to live the life of his uncle the wool merchant and may even have been prevented by his stepmother from garnering the financial and social advantage of living in the family home. Much attention has been focused on Beolco's economic situation, particularly the description of his poverty by Sperone Speroni, who in the *Dialogue on Usury* exclaimed: "My poor Ruzante, is this the bed that you sleep in, one like you who in the art of making rustic comedies have no equal in Italy? This cloak that you put over yourself as a blanket at night, is it not the same that you wear on your back around Padua every day summer and winter? Who takes your boots off in the evening? Who lights the fire in your room? Who draws your water? What do you drink? What do you eat?"[41] Less well known to critics is the assertion of Beolco's follower Giandomenico Maganza (Magagnò) that if the playwright had not found a patron in Cornaro, Padua would not have heard his songs or seen his later comedies "because it's the ruin / of a good brain, when he wants to sing, / to wear himself out in thinking about what he's going to eat."

The financial implications of both passages should be analyzed with caution. As scholars have pointed out recently, Beolco's father did leave him twenty-five ducats. Additionally, Speroni, embroiled in a theological controversy, may have exaggerated Beolco's poverty to counteract an earlier passage that seemed to promote usury.[42] Maganza, requesting patronage for himself, may have overstated the financial importance of the patron. The consistency of the two descriptions, however, indicates that they contain a grain of truth that should be examined through the sixteenth-century lens emphasizing cultured leisure.

The lament of Speroni, who elsewhere stated that gold was as important to a gentleman as a sword to a soldier, was that Beolco's finances did not permit him the gentlemanly status to which his artistic talent entitled him. He had no servant to perform his household chores, he could not wear the latest in fashion or even change his clothes according to the season, and his cloak doubled as a blanket. At a time when Italian society increasingly prized the leisured gentleman (Menegazzo saw this as the reason for Speroni's earlier tolerance of usury) and when a serious split developed even in the upper classes between the very wealthy and others, Beolco's inheritance equaled two years' wages for an infantryman, the lowest army rank.[43] His closeness to the fabulous wealth and power of such Venetian patricians as Molin presented him with abundant evidence of the differences between his life and theirs.

What remained to him was to accept the best patron available, Alvise Cornaro, living in another man's home and doing his bidding, a solution which later plays show to have been problematic. Nancy Dersofi has interpreted Beolco as having taken refuge in the theater. To that I would add that he seems to have done so because life outside it did not allow him the affirmation that he sought. Kept from exercising influence over real-life society, he created a new, liminoid one in his plays, not only legitimating himself and the other excluded but placing them at the center of the social order. His choice of a performance medium allowed him to make direct appeals to those who currently controlled society to espouse his innovations.

Chapter Four

Angry Rebellion

The Prologues of the *Moscheta:* Two Early Versions

Manuscripts, Dates, and Performances. The Marciana miscellany, which has proved such a rich source of Ruzantine materials, contains a fragment of the *Moscheta* consisting of the prologue and the opening of the first act. A second manuscript of the prologue is found in the Verona City Library. Lovarini linked the Marciana text to the 1528 Carnival season in Ferrara, seeing its references to Cremona and Ferrara as alluding to the settings of Ariosto's plays *Necromancer* and *Lena* that, according to available evidence, were performed that year. The Verona prologue contains a reference to a second *prologista;* its absence from the Marciana text led Lovarini to hypothesize that the reference had been deleted by a copyist, and, therefore, that the Marciana manuscript was the later one. Zorzi generally accepted Lovarini's opinion.[1]

Giorgio Padoan questioned the 1528 date of the Ariostan performances and asserted that a 1529 composition would more appropriately explain a reference to famine in the prologue. Such a revision proves untenable, however. Recent scholarship affirms 1528 for the Ariostan performances, and the prologue's aside concerning the famine of "this year" is clearly a disclaimer added to the original message after the famine's onset in late 1527 with the failure of the crop.[2]

Padoan's argument that the Veronese prologue is an expansion of, and thus later than, the Marciana version is more successful. The date of 1530–31 that he assigns it, however, seems precluded by the criticisms of the Spanish. The agreement between Clement VII and Charles V, reached in June 1529 and symbolized in the Pope's coronation of the Spanish king as Holy Roman Emperor, made Charles the virtual ruler of Italy and rendered criticism of him less likely. Such remarks are deleted, in fact, from the prologue of Beolco's *Flora's Play (Fiorina),* which Padoan has shown to be a remake of the Veronese Prologue and which he dates to 1531–32. A comparison of the Marciana and Veronese prologues shows anti-Spanish criticism strong in the first and attenuated in the second, suggesting that they correlate respectively with the strong anti-Imperial feeling after the 1527 Sack of Rome by Imperial troops and its diminution in late 1528 and 1529. Such a development would have been particularly important to Beolco's audience because of the widespread anti-Imperial feeling in northeastern Italy, and Ercole II d'Este's marriage to Renée of France in 1528.

Padoan's suggestion that the Tuscan-language announcer of the Verona text may have been Ariosto is fruitful, especially in light of the prologue's allusion to the prologue of Ariosto's *Lena* (for example, the confusion about what goes in front and what in back). Beolco's rebuke of his colleague apparently refers to the Tuscanization of Ariosto's major work, the *Orlando furioso*, that he was then undertaking (the language in earlier versions had been closer to the poet's native Ferrarese).

The probable dates of the Marciana and Veronese prologues, then, are respectively 1528 and early 1529. The full text of the Marciana fragment probably was the play presented that year in Ferrara. It may also have been the farce recited prior to a dinner given in the same city on 20 May 1529 and described by court cook Cristoforo da Messisbugo.[3] The Verona text (appropriately titled "Intermezzo" in the manuscript) probably served as between-act or mealtime entertainment, such as the recitation given at the seventh course of the same May banquet, where, as Messisbugo notes, Paduan peasant types figured among the entertainers. The hypothesis that they included Beolco is supported by his absence from documents concerning the acquisition of land for Cornaro in a nearby region of the Po Valley, where his presence is recorded both before and after.

Content. The title plays on several allusions: *moschetto* is a pejorative term for the incorrect Italian of dialect speakers attempting to use the standard language based on Florentine. *Mosca* means "fly," explaining the *prologista*'s declaration that if he tried to speak in the Florentine way, he would have flies (*RT*, 687). The term also recalls the Italian expression "a fistful of flies," that is, the results of a useless action. Such, the *prologista* emphatically states, would be his attempt to speak Italian rather than Paduan.

The Marciana prologue begins with the aggressive affirmation that "the world is all turned ass upwards" because neither women nor men wish to follow the natural, preferring instead to overdo. The *prologista* denounces the current trend of adopting Florentine, which is as bad as if he, a Paduan and an Italian, spoke Spanish or German. "But I don't want to, because I know that keeping yourself with your own natural straight, as the Law says, 'delights both of the sexes'" (*RT*, 677).

The speaker volunteers to do the audience a service by teaching the men to get on the right road and the women to let themselves be regulated. His advice is to stick to the natural in language, food, and clothing, as the peasants do. He acknowledges that bread is scarce "this year," but that ordinarily country women are so strong from eating natural foods that if they encountered a man from the city, they would put him underneath them right away. City women, on the other hand, spend so much time fussing with corsets and shawls and skirts that they sometimes take something that should go in front and put it in back, taking the thing out of the natural. They wear rings in their ears, putting a hole where one doesn't belong. "I've even seen those that have overskirts made to keep them wider down below than up above; and that's not attractive at all. I look at our women: the tighter they've got it, the more we like them, and so should every man, I think" (RT, 679). He then chastizes the young bloods for their foppishness in having their breeches slit open on the buttocks, and hanging over the knee.[4] "If it were up to me, I'd make a good law and a new statute: that when someone was from a town and he wanted to talk like he was from another town and overdo, I'd make him lose the wish" (RT, 679).

Praise for the natural and for birds and plants in the countryside follows, as well as the wish that everyone could go around naked so that men and women would get what they wanted when they chose, because there are some guys that seem to be men, but aren't even the half of it. The audience should get behind one another to keep their naturals straight, and go the other way if they see someone going outside the natural. The speaker himself could speak Spanish, and gives an example (actually an approximation of Italian), but it would be flies. He wouldn't change his tongue for two hundred Florentine ones. The audience might get bored with the same old one, however, and look for something else, but they should not exchange their tongue for another. "Rather, I tell you, take another one in your mouth, so that you will have two; and I assure you, that if you like the way I speak, I'll always loan you my tongue" (RT, 681). The *prologista* briefly alludes to the plot of the play, which concerns a peasant who tries to change his language and suffers the consequences. He concludes with an explanation that the scene is not Cremona or Ferrara, but Padua.[5]

Act 1 opens with a speech by Ruzante about his norm in marriage: the woman should rule, the way he lets his wife do. At her instigation, they have come to Padua, where he's had a lot to eat and made a lot of friends, especially among the soldiers. One of them has given him some money to take to someone else, but Ruzante has taken it himself. If the soldier asks him about it, he will lie, and if the soldier threatens him, he will respond by being even more menacing.

The Veronese prologue, while repeating much of the material found in the

Marciana text, exhibits some important differences. Reference is made to another *prologista* whose language is Tuscan. Where the speaker talks about the natural pleasing both sexes, he adds that a bird in the breast is worth three in the bush. He will offer services to his audience individually. Good eating eliminates windiness and dross in the stomach and gives a red and white complexion. To the list of feminine vanities is added the *balzo* (a bunch of fabric held in place by a ribbon at the top of the skirt, distorting the silhouette of the hips).[6] The speaker strengthens his new law by including penalties for men and women, and joins the audience in getting behind one another to keep their naturals straight.

Analysis.   One of the most noteworthy features of the Prologues is the presentation of familiar Ruzantine issues as matters of personal concern to the audience. For example, the *prologista*'s couching of the exaltation of country wholesomeness over city artificiality in terms of the spectators' dress invites them to look down and examine themselves. Their highly refined food, he warns with malicious glee, robs them of the refined appearance necessary to their ardent pursuit of ideal Petrarchan beauty. Beolco's concerns, moreover, seem intensified by Alvise Cornaro's attachment to the sober life, an association that Giovanni Calendoli's recent work underlines. They further recall the plain living preached by medieval and Renaissance religious reform movements, to which Beolco seemed particularly sensitive.[7]

Beolco's awareness of contemporary issues and desire to control them lead him to appropriate civic authority in his program of laws, the addition of sanctions to the Veronese Prologue seeming to anticipate the Paduan sumptuary laws of 1532. In a similarly authoritative spirit, he informs the audience firmly that he is going to teach them how to live right, since they have botched the job themselves, and that he is doing this because he is their brother and he loves them.

The *prologista*'s particular condemnation of earrings may have been linked to their recent transformation from symbols of Jewishness to signs of upper-class female conspicuous consumption, which occurred in tandem with a dramatic inflation of dowries. The latter phenomenon has been interpreted by Stanley Chojnacki as signaling greater influence on the part of aristocratic women, as well as increased economic and personal freedom. The change clearly disturbed Beolco, as the play's preoccupation with power relations between men and women indicates.[8]

Earrings also symbolize the pursuit of luxury goods which, during the lean years of the late 1520s, caused patricians (and others) to become indebted to Jewish moneylenders, a practice which Beolco severely condemned during the middle and late phases of his career. In the process, patricians exchanged places with outsiders, as the migration of earrings from Jewish women to aristocratic women indicates. The outsiders thus achieved a control of society denied to Beolco. This and the increasingly marginal status of illegitimates were possible motivations for his attempts to return to an earlier world in which he could have played a more active role. One suspects too that Beolco's moralizing cloaked both self-condemnation and envy, since his purchase of expensive horses had by then plunged him heavily into debt and prevented him from purchasing finery to rival that of the Este court.

The issue of dominance and submission returns continuously in the texts, couched in sexual metaphors. Like modern rock stars, the *prologista* uses images of sexual relations to enforce intimacy with and control over his audience. Yet the images are contradictory. Though he promises to teach men how to be strong and women how to stay in their place, women in his countryside are on top of both city men and their husbands.[9] They control the couple's money, a detail whose contemporaneity with Beolco's marriage bears noting. Their pecuniary power is made explicit when, in the fragment of act 1, Ruzante mentions a *puta,* usually "girl" or "prostitute," but, in the context, the purse the peasant was commissioned by the soldier to convey.[10] Despite the peasant's declaration that, no matter how hungry he is, he will not bend (*RT,* 685), he closes a blind eye to the trade that his wife plies to get the food and drink he fails to earn, and steals money from a soldier to avoid work.

In the play, thus, the world is being turned upside down: honest labor has no value, peasants move to the cities, men are controlled by their wives, the sexes are indistinguishable, men have sexual relations with other men, the mark of the controlled becomes that of the controller. The parallels with Italian states, which had slipped from being dominators to being dominated, and particularly with Ferrara, where the Duke's wife, as daughter of the late King of France, enjoyed higher status than the Duke,[11] seem more than casual. They are matched by parallels with the recent denial of Beolco's claims to an aristocratic inheritance and loss of invitations to perform in Venice, as well as his financial liability to his patron and, apparently, to his wife.

The *Second Oration*

Manuscript, Date, and Performance. The *Second Oration (Seconda Oratione),* of which only a fragment survives in manuscript form, has provoked little chronological controversy. It celebrates the 1528 raising to the cardinalate of Francesco Cornaro (younger brother of the late bishop of Padua), the result of an aggressive program of family influence whose purpose was "vast accumulations of ecclesiastical preferments."[12] A reference to harvest time places the oration in the month of June, while the orator's statement that he had been on the same spot before indicates that the location was the Villa Barco.

Circumstances had deteriorated greatly since the *First Oration*. The Venetian Republic was being drained by the Wars of Cognac. The loss of the harvest in 1527 and a low yield in 1528 brought famine to the poor, the death toll heightened by the wave of sickness that typically struck those weakened by hunger. Special laws forced all Venetian citizens and corporate groups, a significant portion of mainland property owners, to send their grains to Venice, whose supplies were further augmented by imports from other parts of the Mediterranean basin. While the government allowed some of the accumulation to be parceled out to mainland cities, no provisions seem to have been made for the rural areas, whose inhabitants at most were able to obtain something from speculators. Peasants deserted the countryside and flocked to the cities, where they begged for private charity. The wealthy continued to live extravagantly, scandalizing contemporaries by their pursuit of sumptuous feasts and costly entertainment in the face of the piteous pleas of starving families.[13]

Such short-term sufferings also brought long-term damage to a peasantry living on a margin too slim to absorb the loss. Many peasants sold their property rights, among them a family in Campolongo Maggiore whose purchaser was wealthy Venetian religious reformer Gaspare Contarini. In the village of Rosara, "small leaseholders, proprietors and artisans, those who in the twelfth century had been the heralds and builders of the freedom of the little rural community are now and in this way swallowed up by the mighty estate of a rich Venetian patrician [Alvise Cornaro]."[14] The agent who performed the latter transactions and witnessed the suffering borne by the peasants was Angelo Beolco.

Content. The *Second Oration,* a monologue delivered by a peasant speaker, opens with the declaration that when something is given by nature it is useless to try to stop it because the whole "reversal" (universal) world will help it come into being. An example is the appointment of Cornaro to the cardinalate, which occurred without any effort on his part, and almost against his will. When something must freeze, it will freeze in August.

Explaining that he has come because he was here before, the orator praises the man in whose name that earlier performance took place and whose brotherly love was so great that he died to make room for the new cardinal. Because the old cardinal was boss to the whole Paduan countryside, the orator has come with his brother[15] to celebrate, even deserting the harvest. The rest of

the country people would have come with them, but they are so thin they
could blow away. If he and his brother had not been well foddered for the
winter, the cardinal would have had no one at his party.

The peasants are happy that Cornaro has been made cardinal; it is a sign
that times will get better. They hope that Cornaro will be the good paterfa-
milias of the Gospels, who will get rid of the weeds in the Church's garden,
beginning with Jack of the Lutes (Martinelo da Lautuolo: Martin Luther).
Luther's attraction of so many followers, even in that area, has been taken as
one of the reasons for the present troubles: war, ruin, death, flight. Switching
from the formal *vu* to the familiar *tu,* the orator proves his point by noting
the lack of dancing and singing in the countryside, and the dissolution of
families caused by the centrifugal force of hunger. Even Charity, welcomed
by no one, is forced to roam the world. Returning to the *vu* form, he declares
that people don't fall in love any more because they're afraid of taking on
more expenses.

Christians were about to fall into a stupor when the Cardinal arrived, and
now, like stalks of grain when the sun comes out after a storm, they raise their
heads in hope. Cornaro, in the full flower of his maturity, is strong and able.
God has kept him from marrying so that he may attend to his flock: his
broad cardinal's hat is the perfect accessory for weeding his garden, since it
will shield him from the rain and keep him from freckling. His cloak will
protect the peasants; he will be a mother hen to them, and they his chicks.

Cornaro will soon become pope in the same way he became cardinal. The
orator is so sure of it that he will wager a *tron* (about a ducat, or a month's expenses). "And when that fine day comes that you will be Pope, don't stop
needing me; and if I can do anything, you see, give me the word, act as if I
were your brother, to come and eat and drink together with you and be, you
and me, like good brothers; and you will get some satisfaction out of this, because I'm going to give you some good advice. Now sniff this one and see if it
smells like garlic" (*RT,* 1215).

The list of changes begins with the elimination of the German soldiers,
who started going to Rome for indulgences and soon were descending by the
thousands. To keep them away, the future pope should send cartloads of indulgences over the mountains so the Germans can get them at home. The
second reform concerns the numerous lawsuits that ruin the peasants because
the laws are contradictory and can always be made to favor city people. Instead of the laws of Dato, Bartolo, and Digesto (his approximation of the
codes currently in force) there should be the laws of Menego, Nale, and
Duozo (typical peasant names). "If you will call us [peasants], too, we will

make our own, and if you will make a single law, we will govern ourselves by that one" (*RT,* 1277) and everyone will live in peace.

The third problem, which arises from the violation of the biblical principle that man will live by the sweat of his brow, is that the peasants are not allowed to keep the foodstuffs they produce. Thus they are impoverished and must borrow money from usurers, who, because it is a sin to lend, charge high interest rates. The peasants are ruined and in their anger do a lot of damage that they wouldn't do if they could find bread (a possible reference to the grain tumults of 1528). The solution is to make usury a merit rather than a sin, and to allow Jews to retain their property when they convert to Christianity.[16] In that way, everyone will belong to one flock because to take care of the soul, one must first meet the needs of the body.

The orator concludes by asking Cornaro what he thinks of his advice and assuring him that it is friendly. "And so that you too will know how I know that I'm your friend, I'll tell you. Two that are friends are like two that are pulling on a rope, one at one end and one at the other, and if the first one lets go, the other one falls down. Me now, I know I'm pulling as hard as I can, and I know that if you didn't pull too, I'd end up with my ass on the ground. . . . I want to do something now that I haven't done for more than a year: I want to sing a song and have some fun down here, like the kind of party they're having in Paradise" (*RT,* 1219–21).

Analysis. The *Second Oration,* in the words of Grabher, is characterized by "an intense participation in the cause of the poor, of the oppressed. . . . Here Beolco's voice is raised in a tone that was unusual for its times, and unusual too is the way in which certain evils are represented as a social problem. A problem that, born in the heart, predicts nothing other than a moral revolution in the area of the Gospel."[17] The suffering and death created by the unequal distribution of resources, possibly combined with guilt at the role he played on behalf of the boss who foddered him well, drove Beolco to the liminoid solution of a single law applied uniformly to all.

This most urgent and poignant cry for help on the peasants' behalf is supported by every means of verbal persuasion at Beolco's disposal. The orator first incorporates Cornaro into the liminal world by addressing him as "Your Paternity of you, Most Rebellious Sir Sgardenal," apparently in reference to Cornaro's willful nature and illegitimate son. He also reminds the new prelate of the death of his brother and predecessor, perhaps to imply that Cornaro will eventually be called to account in heaven for how he acquitted himself as bishop. Any offense that Cornaro might take at such boldness is warded off by Beolco's acknowledgment of the old cardinal as boss of the Paduan territory. Finally, there seems to be a tacit appeal to Cornaro's sympathy in the orator's allusion to leaving the harvest. While his declared purpose was to help Cornaro celebrate, he and the prelate were probably aware that other peasants did so to beg for bread.

Having depicted the desperate conditions of the peasants, the orator notes the large numbers of them that have converted to Lutheranism.[18] Though seeing this as a cause of the current trouble, he nonetheless sounds a warning that if the Catholic Church does not attend to the needs of the people, it will lose them to the enemy. Drawing upon his knowledge of aristocratic customs, Beolco then puts peasant misery in terms that Cornaro can understand: things are so bad, they haven't been able to party. The reference to German soldiers would have brought to mind the shocking sack of Rome in 1527 by Imperial troops, perhaps an attempt on Beolco's part to create a solidarity of suffering with Cornaro that would move him to action. The playwright is also willing to use force, delivering his advice with a metaphor ("Sniff this and see if it smells like garlic") that in *Flora's Play* accompanies a punch. The implied violence echoes the popular tumults over grain and anti-Venetian activities among Paduans that had recurred since January.

The concluding recommendations are characterized by the same shrewd techniques of princely counsel that J. H. Hexter observed in the most advanced political thinkers of the time, namely More, Machiavelli and Seyssel: "their common awareness that in politics, general principles usually cooperate through specific institutional structures . . . mere exhortation to a ruler to act this way or that is futile unless there exist institutional structures guiding his action in the desired direction and impeding him from taking alternative directions."[19] Thus Beolco proposes the decentralization of indulgence granting, improvements in the treatment of converted Jews, and a law that accommodates the peasants. He is also perceptive enough to point out the advantages that will accrue to Cornaro from each change.

Beolco couches his appeal in local legal terms. Frequent contact with Venetian patricians had afforded him the opportunity to observe the legal system, one of whose reformers, Luca Tron, attended the 1525 rehearsal. Beolco's orator resembles Venetian lawyers who, as Gaetano Cozzi has observed, played a pivotal role in the justice system because "they had to convince men whose juridical preparation was often rather vague, and who were sensitive, on the other hand, to practical reasoning, which could appeal on the human level; the authoritativeness of their conduct and their oratorical and gesticulative resources were extremely effective instruments."[20]

In his appeal for care of the poor, Beolco appears to draw upon the charitable fervor that was inspired in Venice by the transfer of some Catholic philanthropical institutions there after the Sack of Rome. His strategy, too, seems calculated to appeal to tenets of indigenous piety, "essentially a variant of later medieval Evangelism . . . with its indifference to dogmatic articulation, its openness to personal religious experience and its emphasis on individual responsibility."[21] Beolco's recommendations in the matter of pastoral care reflect a positive approach to contemporary criticisms of clerical failings, which he himself voices in other pieces when he is not asking a prelate for favors. Again, though, they contain the seed of a warning, for dissatisfaction with the clergy was a significant factor leading to the Protestant Reformation.

The proposal to send indulgences to Germany seems to reflect the willingness of some churchmen to permit a limited delegation of authority in that matter, and to align Beolco with the progressive religious thinker Erasmus. It may also, however, have contained an implied criticism of the pope's greed in using the Fugger bank in Rome as a conduit for the lucrative sales of indulgences to Germany, as well as his hiring of German-Swiss soldiers.[22] In either case, the proposal appeals to the church to realize the high price paid by the peasants for its maneuverings.

The seriousness with which Beolco took his responsibilities to the peasants is indicated by his choice of the final metaphor of the rope, which hints, moreover, that he had promised the poor devils whose land rights he was buying that he would appeal to his powerful friends to support them. The appeals to Cornaro as buddy and brother, the heavy-handedness of the threats and references to the damage suffered by the Church, and the impact of the tug-of-war all convey a sense of urgency that reflects a personal commitment on the part of a man who had experienced the loss of self-respect accompanying financial straits.

The *Witty Dialogue*

Date and Performance. The *Witty Dialogue (Dialogo facetissimo)*, despite its misleading title, also centers on the sufferings brought by the famine, though it holds out some hope for future improvement. The first edition (the play does not exist in manuscript form) bore the legend "Performed at Fosson during the hunt in the year of the famine 1528," traditionally interpreted according to the common method of changing years on January 1. Giorgio Padoan, however, noting that the events of the play seem to occur after those of the *Second Oration,* has posited that the inscription reflects the Venetian custom of changing the year on March 1, a hypothesis that shifts the date to 1529. Among the new possibilities created by the change is that the *Dialogue* was the play performed at Ferrara on January 24 of that year, as it corresponds to the description given by Cristoforo da Messisbugo.[23]

A date of 1529 would reinforce Giovanni Calendoli's theory that the play formed part of Alvise Cornaro's campaign to be named administrator of the bishopric of Padua by Cardinal Francesco Pisani.[24] Sanudo reports that Cornaro sent the cardinal the game caught at an extensive hunt held at Fosson in January of the next year, after he had achieved the nomination. A detail of the play that may have been particularly calculated to please Pisani was the espousal of Tuscan language and high culture by two characters, Zaccarotto and the Cornaro-like Priest of Diana, which would have appealed to the taste for things Tuscan among some Venetian patricians and attenuated the association of Zaccarotto and other members of Cornaro's circle with Paduan rebels.

Discussion of the play is complicated by the likelihood, suggested by Lovarini and endorsed by Zorzi, that the play was modified by Cornaro, who is known to have elaborated upon the *First Oration* and who probably readied the text for the printer.[25] His intervention may have been provoked by the *Witty Dialogue*'s direct questioning of the relationship between peasants and landowners. Although the lack of manuscripts precludes a sure answer, there is convincing circumstantial evidence. The obsession with the dead is similar to that characterizing Cornaro's reworking of the *First Oration,* which includes several of the same figures. The Priest of Diana closely resembles Cornaro, who, in Lovarini's opinion, played the part. The theory of good living promoted by Zaccarotto corresponds to Cornaro's *Sober Life,* whose fame in English-speaking countries reached even Andrew Jackson.

Such a possibility is consonant with a program of self-advertisement that manifested itself in Cornaro's progressive falsification of his age (seen as proof of the efficacy of the sober life), the writing of his own funeral eulogy for his grandson to read, and the exaggeration of improvements brought to the village of Codevigo by his plan of agricultural development. Similarly, the grandson's (possibly false) account of Cornaro's habit of producing plays in a theater that he constructed on his hunting grounds enhances Cornaro's prestige through its appeal to a rhetorical ideal.[26] In the same vein, Cornaro may have included the date of the play's performance in its printed version to point out that his efforts to court Pisani would soon succeed. In light of such considerations, scholarly interpretations of the *Witty Dialogue* as proving Beolco's voluntary allegiance to Cornaro's program should be taken with care.

Plot and Characters.   Mentioned in the *Second Oration* as the peasants whose laws should be enacted, Menego, Duozo, and Nale return as protagonists in the *Witty Dialogue.* Menego opens the play with a count of the famine-stricken months that stretch out until the harvest, proposing that the peasants stopper "the hole down below" so they won't be hungry so often. When Duozo optimistically reminds him of the proverb that "the year makes do with what it has" and predicts a good harvest, Menego counters that the usurers will make it fail by stockpiling grain to get even higher prices the next year. They are "greedier for the blood of poor people than a skinny mare for new grass" (*RT*, 695).[27]

The two friends predict that the country people, so hungry that they look like dead men hung in a smokehouse, will eat weeds and field flowers to keep body and soul together until the harvest. Menego worries that his weakness will keep him from the work he needs to survive, noting that it already has affected his love life. Duozo hints that Menego's girlfriend Gnua has another suitor who is threatening to steal her, but Menego brushes him off with the assurance that he will defend her with his sword. His tendency to replace unpleasant reality with pleasant fantasy recurs in the next scene, where he attempts to attract Gnua by offering her a piece of bread he doesn't have, then distracts her by proposing that they sing a duet.

Gnua's suitor Nale arrives, brandishes his sword and challenges the cowering Menego, who allows himself to be beaten. After his rival has left with the girl, Menego calls for a priest to hear his confession before he dies. At the sound of his voice, Duozo rushes back on the scene and receives a tongue-lashing for desertion. Duozo protests that he was unarmed, and points out that Menego didn't draw his own sword, to which Menego replies that he forgot. The quarrel over who was the greater coward continues until Menego loudly asserts that he is on the edge of death. Duozo promises to bring a local magician who serves Diana, goddess of the hunt, to heal him, and departs.

Alone, Menego despairs of his injuries, worrying that no one will ever hire him as a day laborer again. Convinced that he will die either of hunger or of his wounds, he determines to kill himself in such a way that Duozo, whom he believes betrayed him, will be blamed and banished. He is in a quandary as to how to achieve his goal, having given Duozo his sword for protection. In the end, Menego decides to kill two birds with one stone: if he eats himself, he will die with a full stomach. He asks God to forgive him for the sin of killing himself so young and for his only other sin, that of stealing, which he committed to stay alive.

Just as Menego changes his method to strangulation, Duozo returns, bringing with him the Priest of Diana. When the priest heals Menego immediately, Menego eagerly asks him to find bread and get his girlfriend back. Speaking in Tuscan, the priest replies that Menego can have whatever he wants. Duozo assures Menego that the priest is powerful because on their way "he showed me the experience" (*RT*, 711), and puts in his own request for news of their deceased friend Zaccarotto. The priest responds by summoning the soul of Zaccarotto, who, as a follower of Diana, can meet with them only where hunts occur.

Zaccarotto, who also speaks Tuscan, explains that he has been entirely transformed. While he still hunts, his is a different pursuit from that held on earth. When his comrades react with surprise at his freedom to participate in the sport, he assures them that all the good pleasures enjoyed on earth exist in Paradise. The peasants observe wryly that this is not what their priest tells them. The reason for the latitude, according to Zaccarotto, is that righteous men are few and should be encouraged to come, and stay, in Paradise. Thus those who have been prudent in eating and drinking, have treated women with propriety, have been wise stewards of their goods, and have been kind are allowed a paradise where they can eat and drink and do what they want. There is a second Paradise for those who have fasted, abstained, and prayed on earth. There they can continue those activities, and their pleasure consists of the contemplation of God. The peasants agree that the first paradise is the one for them and that they fully qualify for admission.

Menego asks Zaccarotto for news of several other members of Cornaro's circle who have died. He hears that sad Scrinzi has gone to the second place, but cheery Uncle Paul and Pacalono dwell in the heaven of pleasures. Menego and Duozo ask about how the famine and the war will go. Zaccarotto consoles them: they will survive, though not without going hungry. There will be no plague but many women will die in childbirth. While there will be a few more months of war, they will be followed by a long peace, and the harvest will be good.

The mention of food prompts Menego to ask what types are available up there and how they are grown and harvested. Zaccarotto's reply that no work is needed to produce food delights him, and he asks again what type of man is allowed into that heaven. Zaccarotto emphasizes the ability to add to wealth, to use every hour in productive activity, to improve the land, to cultivate good men as friends and welcome their advice, and to be cheerful. The spell is broken by the Priest of Diana, who must attend to his goddess's plans for a great hunt. Before he departs, he prays for the return of Gnua.

Nale appears and apologizes to Menego; he is forgiven, and the two shake hands. Gnua approaches Menego joyfully, offering a kiss. The priest promises them that the goddess Diana will provide for her faithful followers by making this area their exclusive hunting preserve. Young men and women accompanied by musicians approach the peasants, and the play concludes with a dance.

Analysis.   Critical discussion of the *Witty Dialogue* is made difficult by Cornaro's probable intervention, to which Zorzi attributes the mediocrity long seen as the play's distinguishing feature. The present discussion will attempt to focus on those aspects of the *Dialogue* that seem most consonant with Beolco's other work, while recognizing that interpretations concern the play only, and not Beolco as playwright.

Like the *Pastoral,* the *Dialogue* contrasts two levels of society, and their respective languages and cultures. The rural misery eloquently evoked in the opening scenes recalls the *Second Oration*'s condemnation of the upper classes, who strip the peasants of the fruits of their labors.[28] As Paolo Sambin has noted, the portrait of the usurers raises the question of whether the peasants saw Cornaro in that role rather than the benevolent one of the Priest of Diana. The realization that usurers and city people wield ultimate control seems to lie at the heart of Menego's defeatism, manifested in his inability to defend himself, despite his boasts.

City and country cultures are connected by a passageway, however, which is discovered by Menego. Irritated at being asked to help remember the name of the hunting goddess, a subject he knows nothing about, he begins to list the folk names and stars. He hits on Diana, a name which, like *pan* (bread/ Pan) of the *Pastoral,* initiates a series of paired references to classical and peasant culture.

Ancient myths are recalled in various ways. The transformation of Zaccarotto seems to conflate the stories of Actaeon and Orion. The former was a huntsman who, having discovered the virginal Diana at her bath, was punished by being turned into a stag and devoured by his own dogs. Orion, beloved of the goddess, was unintentionally murdered by her; when she discovered her error, she turned his lifeless body into a constellation. The healing of Menego parallels in many ways that of Hippolytus, revived by Aesculapius at the behest of Diana when she learned that he had been unjustly killed. Ippolito, the Italian version of the name, belonged to a member of the powerful Este family of Ferrara, in whose territory the hunt and the probable second presentation of the play took place.

The expression "seeing the experience" resembles the terminology of Renaissance peasant cults in which Diana was the goddess both of fertility and of its opposite, death. She conducted souls back and forth between this world and the next, and led the souls of the premature and violent dead on a "wild hunt."[29] On the Feast of the Dead (2 November) 1525, Angelo Beolco cowitnessed with Giacomo Zaccarotto a farm contract between a villager and the Cornaro brothers. On that occasion, Beolco and his friend were likely to have been reminded of the custom, practiced throughout most of Italy, of providing food, beverages, and resting places for the dead when they return home on their feast. A comparison of the *Witty Dialogue*'s two heavens with the religious appeals of the *Second Oration* reveals an important difference. In the earlier piece, Beolco had exhorted Cardinal Cornaro to bring about Christ's kingdom on earth. In the latter one, the conventional heaven where God is contemplated is reserved for losers. The preferable, entirely secular, paradise of pleasures contains no reference to a divine being. Rather, it recalls Virgil's description of the pagan Elysius in book 6 of the *Aeneid*, is attained by following a pagan goddess, and rings with the laughter and song of comedians.[30] One is tempted to see Beolco's evident disillusionment with Christianity as the product of the ruthless disregard for the rights of the poor by the wealthy, typified by the coldblooded acquisition of their property by Cornaro and religious reformer Gaspare Contarini.

The *First Dialogue (The Veteran)*

Date, Manuscripts, and Performances. Printed together in the sixteenth century under the collective title *Two Dialogues of Ruzzante in the Rustic Tongue,* the next two very brief works function as a unit in a number of ways. The *First Dialogue,* entitled *Dialogue of Ruzante Back from the Front,* is found in two manuscripts, the Marciana miscellany and the Veronese manuscript containing the *First Oration.* Italian critics have shortened the title to *The Speech* or *The Veteran,* the latter of which will be used here as it captures the sense of the play succinctly. The *Second Dialogue* or *Bilora* (the name of the protagonist, here translated as "Weasel"), was the first of Ruzante's plays to be translated into English, followed by the *First Dialogue* (under the title *Ruzzante Returns from the Wars*). They remain the only works available in English.[31]

Questions about dating and performances of *The Veteran* have vexed critics for a number of years. Emilio Lovarini at first believed it to be a later version of the play performed in Venice in 1520 because of Sanudo's reference to Ruzante and Menato. Of the three plays containing those names, Lovarini chose *The Veteran* because the *Moscheta* was later and *The Woman from Ancona* too long. He later observed that a reference in the play to the departure of the cardinal was the single clue to its date, placing it at November 1521. Noting the number of allusions to the Wars of Cambrai, Ludovico Zorzi on the other hand posited a date of approximately 1515.[32] There are other early references beyond those observed by Zorzi. The route followed by Ruzante in returning from the battlefield replicates that taken in 1509 by the

Venetian army after Agnadello, with the exception of the passage through Cremona, which was lost to the Venetians until 1515.[33] Moreover, Ruzante's excuse for his flight, that he as squadron leader was at the back of the field and the retreat of other men kept him from entering the fray, is identical to that of captain-general Niccolò Orsini for his abstention from Agnadello, an important factor in the historic defeat.

Giorgio Padoan has undertaken a revision of the chronology, based on references which he has linked to the Wars of Cognac, and specifically to the second half of 1529.[34] While the sum of his argument is convincing, some points are not as strong as they might appear. Padoan states that Beolco uses the formula "sbreseghegi da Robin" for the only time in this work, which he consequently dates to the period after 1523 when Francesco Maria Della Rovere, Duke of Urbino (many of whose troops hailed from the mountainous region near Brisighella), was given charge of the Venetian infantry. His point, however, is undermined by the reference in the *First Oration* (1521) to "sbrisighiegi o politani da Robin" (*RT*, 1193), which Padoan himself notes but does not take into consideration. A past remote verb tense referring to Agnadello does not necessarily place the battle years earlier, as both Menato and Ruzante use the past remote to refer to actions of no more than four months before. Venetian armies' pillaging of their own peasants' resources did not originate in the Wars of Cognac, but involved those of the second decade of the century as well. The peasant attitude linking military service with material reward rather than patriotism was not new; as Grabher noted, it may be found in late fifteenth-century sonnets published by Lovarini.[35]

Padoan concludes his article with the hypothesis that *The Veteran* may have been an anonymous play given in Venice during the Carnival of 1530, which Sanudo notes extremely briefly. The hypothesis forms part of a larger theory that Beolco returned to Venice after the 1526 dinner, other evidence for which has been shown to be inaccurate.[36] Working against such an identification is Ruzante's pilgrimage in the play to the ancient church of San Fantin in Venice with its long-venerated miraculous image of the Virgin, a church that at the time was nonexistent because under reconstruction during the playwright's entire career.[37] That Beolco would probably have been aware of such a matter is demonstrated in *The Girl from Piove*, in which a newly finished church serves as the setting for some important scenes. The allusion thus seems to function like the statements in prologues of such plays as the *Moscheta* which tell the audience the name of the city, probably necessitated by the generic nature of the stage cityscape. It was probably intended, therefore, not for a Venetian audience minutely informed of the state of the reconstruction, but for inhabitants of another city who identified the healing powers of the famous shrine with Venice.

Available evidence, then, points to the play's having first been written in about 1515, for a performance in Padua, and revised in 1529.[38] The extant version's strong anti-Venetian tone and mockery of the hasty and undignified retreat of Venetian general Bartolomeo d'Alviano seem suited to a presentation in Venice's traditional rival, Ferrara, which in the 1529 Peace of Bologna gained important concessions from the republic. The abbreviated structure, which critics have linked with Erasmus's *Dialogues,* seems appropriate to the between-course entertainment that Beolco and his troupe provided there, and the play thus may have been performed at the May 1529 banquet.

Plot and Characters. A distraught Ruzante arrives in Venice in search of his wife Gnua.[39] He curses wars and soldiers and swears that he will never return to the battlefield. He has covered the one hundred and eighty (actually about one hundred) miles from Cremona in three days, driven by fear and attracted by desire. He ran so fast that he lost the sole of the shoe he had stolen from a peasant as part of his booty. Worried that he may be dreaming, he reassures himself of the reality of his location by recalling his boat journey from the mainland and his trip to San Fantin to fulfill a vow. A new fear that he is not really alive is assuaged by a bite into a piece of bread. Imagining that his wife will tremble at his soldierly appearance, he admits to himself that he had to be dragged kicking and screaming to military service. Then, anticipating the questions that his pal (Menato) will ask about the battlefield, he rouses himself with a glowing account of his prowess. Seeing his friend, Ruzante calls out.

Menato observes that he looks as bad as a hanged man, and, disappointed, Ruzante counters with a series of excuses about the difficulties of military life that range from heavy helmets to poor food and drink. His language has been deformed by his military companions, the Brisighellesi from Urbino. Fear taught him in one day to understand French insults, which he can still reel off. The less-tutored Menato mistakes one for a claim that peasants don't pay for their houses, and swiftly retorts that they pay dearly, to which Ruzante adds that the *paron* (landowners or, more generally, the rich and powerful) should be hung (*RT,* 521). Complimented by Menato on his overcoat, he confides that he stole it from a *villano,* and goes on to complain that the *villani* out there are so stingy they would let you freeze to death for a nickel. Menato responds dryly that now that Ruzante is a soldier, he thinks he's not from the *villa* (country). Backpedaling swiftly, Ruzante protests that he called them *villani* because they lack the manners of the Paduans; a *villano* is one who acts villainously, not someone who comes from the *villa.*

Menato quizzes Ruzante about his military experience, particularly his lack of booty, prisoners, and combat scars. Ruzante prevaricates with stories about wage months of one hundred days, bread that sprouts lice, and wine that gives scabs. He claims that he was all set to fight but, since he was a corporal, he was at the back of the field and, when those in front of him turned to flee, he, as a gentleman, had to do so as well. The cross on his chest was red on one side and white on the other so that he could turn it over and mingle with the enemy. He had to look to his salvation, since one can do nothing against many. In the heat of battle, everyone cries out, and you look for a way out, then you see someone escaping get shot in the back, so it takes a lot of courage even to flee. Even Sir Bortolamio, who was such a big shot in Vicenza, jumped in the water and hightailed it back to Padua.[40] As for booty, Ruzante explains, he was unlucky.

Menato is curious to know how far afield his friend got. Ruzante replies that he was at the devastated battlefield of Ghiaradadda (Agnadello), where you could see nothing but "sky and the bones of dead men" (*RT,* 529). Menato asks about the people there, almost as one might have asked about the inhabitants of Hiroshima after the atomic bomb. Ruzante describes them as being like Paduan peasants, although they talk a little funny: they are baptized, they make bread, they eat, they get married, they have children, they fall in love "but it's true that this war and the soldiers have made love leave out the ass" (*RT,* 529).

Ruzante soon brings the conversation around to Gnua who, according to Menato, hooked up with some of the cardinal's grooms after her husband enlisted. When they left, she went to Venice and found herself some real lowlifes. She refuses to recognize him anymore, and, he is sure, Ruzante will receive the same treatment. He had better watch out for her boyfriends, too. The veteran, bragging of his valor, assures his friend that there is no danger and that Gnua will welcome him.

When Gnua appears, she berates Ruzante for returning with nothing for her and urges him to leave so that he will not ruin her present luck. When he pleads, she explains that she has to eat every day, a need he is unable to satisfy.[41] She admits: "It's not you that I hate, it's your misfortune; because I would like to see you rich, so that we could have a good time together, you and I" (*RT,* 535). When Gnua asserts that his four months of service have amounted to nothing, he counters abjectly, "I haven't bothered you for the last four months (*RT,* 535). But Gnua's tirade continues as, joined by Menato, she complains that he bears no marks of battle.

Preparing to leave, she spots her lover and tells Ruzante to let her go. He clings to her desperately, his warning that he will no longer let himself be led around by the nose discounted by Menato, who assures Gnua that Ruzante will not kill her. Gnua bitterly rejoins, "Let him kill the lice all over him" (*RT,* 539). Gnua's strongman, with the silence of a sure victor, beats Ruzante, then leaves.

The concluding scene reprises the *Witty Dialogue,* with Ruzante blaming his companion for not defending him against so many and Menato repeating that there was only one and that Ruzante should have been able to defend himself. Ruzante finally takes refuge in the explanation that Gnua is a witch and has used a spell to produce the vision of many attackers. Resolving at first to burn her, he fantasizes a better punishment. He would have tied her and her lover together "and the I would have made them . . . Do you get it?" (*RT,* 543). Menato, remarking that he is laughing like it was a joke, or a comedy, or like he had been to a wedding, is unable to comprehend his friend's obliviousness to the real import of the episode. Ruzante concludes, "Hey, pal. What's it to me? Oh, the clap, it would have been something to laugh at, if I tied them up" (*RT,* 543). In one version he adds the line, "So then you would have told me not to make any more comedies."

Analysis.   *The Veteran's* most powerful interpreter is Carlo Grabher, who sees the character Ruzante transported into a nightmare world where the real and the unreal merge in and out of one another, the boundaries between them, like those between sanity and insanity, dissolved by the inhumanity of war and grinding poverty.[42] The desperate stoicism with which Ruzante faces the destruction around him belies the cleverness of equal desperation with which he finds ways to cling to life. His final disappointment lies in rejection by his wife, to whom, despite her own lack of principles and even sympathy, he is tied by "an elementary conjugal right to which, however, is added the submission to a certain female charm and the humble and subdued attachment of one who has no one else." Ruzante's final hysterical, humiliated laughter is directed, more than at the horror of the situation, at his own inability to change it.

Here Beolco's work reflects not only the passing destruction of an individual war, but the lasting destruction of Italian hopes for hegemony. Most Italian city-states would henceforth be directly dominated by larger nation-states. Venice, the most fortunate, found her conquest of both sea and land empires checked. She had faced the humiliation of the enemy's arrival at her doorstep, and the need to abjectly plead for the Emperor's mercy. More importantly, she had confronted the weakness of her own ruling class's passivity and addiction to luxury in the teeth of the crisis, and suffered the outrage of having to sell government offices to raise desperately needed cash.[43] In future years, the republic would be able to maintain her liberty in the formal sense but (with a few exceptions) not with masculine aggressiveness. Like Gnua, she would do so by seducing those brawnier than she, pursuing a policy of manipulative diplomacy.

In an unusual coincidence of public and private cycles, Beolco simultaneously found himself confronting his own cowardice and hypocrisy.[44] The champion of the peasants, he now found himself, like Ruzante, in the service of a Venetian lord. Just as Ruzante stole a few pieces of clothing as part of his military pay, Beolco, bereft of resources, despoiled the small leaseholders of Rosara of their meager possessions. Gnua, the personification of money, had, like his inheritance, attached herself to a Venetian who wielded power. The shrill laughter generated by the mounting tension between self-interest and altruism, between the drive for self-affirmation and need to survive, rings maniacally at the expense not only of Ruzante but of Beolco.

The *Second Dialogue (Weasel)*

Date, Manuscripts, and Performances. The *Second Dialogue* exists only in printed form. No record of performances survives, although the strongly anti-Venetian tone of the play is consonant with Cornaro's circle in Padua and the Este court at Ferrara. The latter hypothesis is supported by the existence of a modified version of the play in the archives of Modena, which house most of the Este papers (including the only known document in Beolco's hand, a letter to Ercole II). Because the play depicts a time of greater prosperity (at least for the city characters) and Bilora (Weasel) refers to his soldiering in the past, Padoan has dated the play about 1530.[45]

Plot and Characters. Like *The Veteran*, the final version of the *Moscheta*, and the later *Flora's Play* and *The Girl from Piove*, *Weasel* opens with a breathless monologue delivered by a love-crazed peasant (Weasel). As ardent and single-minded as his namesake in pursuit of its prey, Weasel has followed his wife Dina from the country to Venice, where she is living with a rich, elderly Venetian merchant (Andronico). Weasel blames his dangerous journey on love, whose power is so great that it has even worked on the old man: "May the clap eat him up, him and the guy who brought him to my town, Shylock that he is! I hope he never gets a chance to have any happiness out of his money, or enjoy it any more, like he keeps me from doing with my wife" (*RT,* 549). It was while he was off towing boats to earn some money that his wife was "towed" away from him. Starving, he hopes at least to beg a piece of bread from her.

An old friend, Pitaro, happens on the scene. He is none too happy to see Weasel, who, after stumbling over the words, finally asks him if he knows anything about "Sir Androtene."[46] Pitaro replies that the old man lives right in the neighborhood, and asks Weasel's intentions. Weasel confides that he really doesn't like to fight and that he would prefer to reach an agreement rather than go to court. He would be willing to let bygones be bygones if the old man would give him some money and return his woman. If they were outside Venice, things would go differently, but in the city the old man could have him drowned in a ditch (as Weasel terms Venice's canals).

Pitaro praises his friend's wisdom, recommending that he address the Venetian with soft words and lavish titles of respect, foregoing his tendency to bully. Weasel accepts the advice, although he would rather "fling him to the ground like a spitball" (*RT*, 553). The best plan, Pitaro adds, would be to go now because Dina is alone in the house. Faced with the actualization of his schemes, Weasel becomes less sure of himself, asking Pitaro if she really will come back. His friend vacillates, saying that she might, but then describing her present situation of comfort and power. Pitaro leaves to run an errand. Weasel hesitates in front of Dina's door but, feeling love stir within him, knocks.

Thinking he is a beggar, Dina brushes him off. When he identifies himself, she slips out to meet him, though first obtaining assurances that he will not beat her. She complains bitterly about the sickly old man's disgusting advances, but hesitates when Weasel invites her to return home, saying that the old man doesn't want her to, and that she really is having a good time. Infuriated, Weasel threatens to bring down (blaspheme) the saints, but finally accepts Dina's proposal to return later to speak with Andronico. When he asks for bread, she instead gives him coins and sends him to the local tavern.

The subsequent soliloquys by the two rivals reveal the differences in their personalities and experiences. Weasel, stopping to count the coins, remembers that the two-bit piece was the first one he spent when he fell in love. He then evaluates the other coins and plans how he will spend them. Andronico, on the other hand, recalls that when he was young, he was too serious, and wise men of his acquaintance urged him to find a girl and fall in love, warning that if he waited until he was old he would do something foolish. Regretting that his body does not always respond to his intent, he cheers himself with the thought that love has managed to make him take this girl away from her husband, though at the risk of his life. He enthuses about her sensuous beauty, then worries about what will happen if a relative tries to come and take her back. Reminding himself that he has made up his mind to enjoy her, he ennumerates the ways in which he spoils her. If she knows how to handle him properly, he hints, he will leave her most of his estate.

Shortly after Andronico enters his house, Weasel returns from the tavern and meets Pitaro. They agree that Pitaro will approach Andronico, and Weasel warns: "And listen, if you see that he's pulling back, tell him by the blood of Cripes that she has a husband who's as bad as the clap: 'that if you don't give her back to him, he will kill you'" (*RT,* 565). Pitaro, however, addresses Andronico (with whom he is already acquainted, as Andronico's spontaneous use of his name indicates) with a confidential yet respectful air. He urges the old man to put himself in the husband's shoes, noting that the youthful Dina "is not a pot for your ladle" (*RT,* 569). Andronico rages that he will never leave Dina, certainly not to let her go back to her good-for-nothing husband, who gives her more beatings than bread. He has gone about in armor all summer to protect himself, and now her husband must take care of his needs another way. After several increasingly angry exchanges, Pitaro proposes that they call Dina and ask her. Confident that she will choose him, Andronico agrees.

Protected from the effects of Weasel's anger, Dina reviles him for beating her every day, and swears that she will never return to him. Pitaro loses his temper and tells Andronico that not a half hour earlier she had promised that she would return home. Dina denies everything. Telling her to go to her room, Andronico asks Pitaro if he wishes anything else. Pitaro confides that Weasel is up to no good and Andronico would do well to give Dina up. Andronico exclaims that he will not be threatened, and that he is prepared to beat Pitaro if he sees him when he goes out again. After the merchant has closed the door, Pitaro retorts, "And be gone with the wind, so that I never see you again!"

When Weasel hears how things have gone, he berates his friend for his ineffectuality. Pitaro, who has had enough, tells him that he should have helped out if he didn't like what was happening and asks if Weasel is going to beat him. Weasel demurs, then turns down an invitation to accompany Pitaro. Left alone, he rails at the way everything is turned upside down. Since he is ruined for life, he will get rid of the old man and then leave. To keep his anger from getting the better of him and ruining his plan, he rehearses how he will attack Andronico. Pulling out his hunting knife,[47] he pretends that his wine jug is his rival. "I will begin by blaspheming and bringing down all the Christ-have-mercies there are in Padua, and the Blessed Mother, and God-be-with-you." After violently cursing Andronico, he will drive his knife into him again and again "until I have killed him" (*RT,* 575–77). His preparation complete, Weasel stations himself by Andronico's house to wait.

Hearing the loud skirmishing, Andronico steps out, wishing that he were a chief of the night patrol so he could give the noisemaker his due. As he sets off on the errand, Weasel jumps him, as he did in his rehearsal, stabbing him repeatedly. Andronico cries out for help, says that he is dying, then falls silent. Standing over the body, Weasel exclaims, "Give me my woman now. You should have let her be. Well, now, I think he's dead, I do. His legs and feet aren't jumping. Boy, he's kicked the bucket, he has. My God, good-bye! He's shat the grapevines, he has. Didn't I tell you?" (*RT,* 579).

Analysis. The singularity of *Weasel* has been recognized by critics Nino Borsellino and Guido Davico Bonino, the latter of whom has defined its onstage murder as "the only one, perhaps, in [Italian] sixteenth-century comedy."[48] Moreover, the murder inverts the social order. The danger inherent in such an ending may explain Beolco's interposing of a further double mask between himself and his character by changing Ruzante's name to Bilora and declining, for the only time in his career, to play the protagonist's role himself (it was assigned to an actor named Castegnola). Paul Grendler has observed that Renaissance writers often omitted the names of the targets of their criticism out of fear of retaliation. Beolco—aware, like Weasel, that he could be executed for his actions—went further and masked the character uttering the criticism.

Perhaps wishing to provide an ampler justification for his revolutionary views, Beolco apparently drew on other texts as sources. Some aspects of the play appear inspired by the *Tyrannicide* of Lucian of Samosata, an ancient satirist known for his questioning of authority. In 1516, Aldus Manutius printed the Latin translation of the *Tyrannicide* that More and Erasmus had produced ten years earlier. It may have been these Northern European thinkers who brought the politically dangerous implications of Lucian's thought (which had previously escaped the attention of Italian humanists) to the attention of Beolco and his contemporaries.[49]

Weasel's justification of his violence, that Andronico had illegally taken his wife, is congruent with a philosophy that originated in Luther's *Of Temporal Authority: to What Extent it Should be Obeyed* (1523) and took final shape in Philipp Melancthon's *Instruction Concerning Self-Defense* (1547). In Luther Peterson's characterization, the latter text holds that "reason enabled men to recognize when rulers inflicted atrocious injury (*atrox iniuria*) on their subjects. In such a circumstance, and if no magistrate should step in with help, natural law permitted (*erleubet*) one to defend himself and 'there are many cases' where this commanded (*geboten*) husbands to protect their wives, fathers their children, and magistrates their subjects."[50]

The play offers a number of clues to those constructing a theory accounting for its break with social and literary norms. These include the Cornaro-like characteristics of Andronico, the equation of the merchant's enjoyment of his money with Weasel and Dina's enjoyment of each other, and Weasel's anticipation of the murder. While critics (including the present writer in earlier works) have referred to this last episode as a fantasy, a close reading of the text shows it to be a rehearsal. That the protagonist is rehearsing not for a play but for a future action provides support for the widespread interpretation of Beolco's plays as unusually closely tied with real life.

When linked with Beolco's biography, these clues produce the impression that Weasel, who drove Dina into the arms of old Andronico through his violence, parallels Beolco, who drove his small inheritance to Cornaro through reckless spending. As Weasel showed his reluctance to go to court and his willingness to reach an agreement if his rights were given minimal recognition, so Beolco agreed to work out a friendly settlement with his father's heirs rather than sue. When Andronico did not respond, Weasel attacked, as Beolco must have in 1533 when his uncle desisted from his efforts to stop Angelo's collection of his settlement so as not to litigate (or quarrel: *litigare*) with his nephew.[51] Weasel obtained money from his estranged wife; Beolco paid his debts with his in-laws' few precious goods. In both cases, financial straits combined with personal volatility produced an explosion of violence against a figure who represented the ability of the authority structure to constrain the action of the individual.

Horses occupy a central place in the lives of both character and author. Beolco, not unlike his father who had pawned the family valuables to buy a horse to take him to Tuscany, squandered his severance money on expensive horses. Weasel planned to buy a horse with the coat he would take from Andronico. The critical issue thus appears to have been independence, the horse in the Renaissance having much the same significance as the car in the twentieth century. That independence had been appropriated by the "usurers" (as Weasel labelled Andronico), whom Beolco had identified as early as the *Pastoral* with the upper class that made all the laws to its advantage and siphoned off the food produced by peasant labor. Here there are clear parallels between the social role of illegitimate sons, increasingly marginalized during the sixteenth century, and that of the peasants, whose financial and political self-determination also grew more limited. Just as Dina was drawn to the wealthy Andronico, land, goods, money and political power were passing into the hands of a limited group of patricians, like Andronico also more inclined to pursue life's pleasures.[52] This group included the aristocratic Venetian hosts of Beolco's early career, who supported him when they were young and outside the power structure, but who withdrew from him as they became more established and he more radical.

An overview of the plays considered in the present chapter indicates that Beolco's efforts to dismantle the system of privilege intensified during the troubled times of the late 1520s. In the *Second Oration,* he had presented the peasants' right to justice in the most compelling terms, approaching Cardinal Cornaro as one responsible Christian to another. When he failed to achieve social equality with this strategy, he began to entertain pagan solutions (the *Witty Dialogue*). The failure of this second attempt produced *Weasel's* explosive leveling of the old system (against which the heavenly pillars of authority Mary and God were helpless) and its substitution with the egalitarian, nonreligious justice of the new one.

A comparison of Beolco's solution with Boccaccio's is, again, illuminating. In the *Decameron's* fourth day, Ghismonda (4.1) and Isabetta (4.5) rebel against the abuse of natural rights by figures of authority, specifically the refusal of their male guardians to contract marriages for them. They both take lovers, who are killed by the guardians in a reassertion of their authority. Ghismonda then chooses suicide as her only means of self-affirmation, while Isabetta dies of a broken heart. In *Weasel,* on the contrary, the dissenter kills the authority figure. By removing the usurer whose arrival in the village unbalanced his life, Weasel both restores equilibrium and creates a new social order based on universal natural rights, one that is inspired by a mythical past and anticipates a better (though distant) future.

The play thus offers support for Turner's theory as it contributes to a modified version of the Burckhardtian thesis that the Renaissance, with its stress on the individual, initiated the modern era in Western culture.[53] While historical research has recently affirmed the continuity of many social and political institutions from the Middle Ages to the Renaissance, an analysis of literary and artistic production (which formed the bulk of Burckhardt's evidence) demonstrates the existence of a qualitative change, one in which Beolco pioneered by rejecting traditional elitism and insisting that recognition of individual rights and development of individual talents be extended to all, while affirming that government is the embodiment of both self-empowerment and mutual obligation.

Chapter Five

The Forked Tongue of Power

The *Moscheta:* A Mouthful of Flies

Date and Performance. The complete version of the *Moscheta,*[1] which survives only in sixteenth-century printings, has been assigned by Padoan to about 1532.[2] Although no records of performances have been discovered, the general history of Beolco's career as well as internal references to Padua and Ferrara point to its having been performed in those two cities. Written and revised over the course of Beolco's middle period (see chapter 4: "The Prologues of the *Moscheta:* Two Early Versions"), the play encloses it like parentheses, moving from the earlier sense of outer attack and inner conflict to the later mood of isolation and social duality.

Plot and Characters. The prologue blames marital infidelity on the irresistible force of women's natures and men's naturals, which make them do things they would not otherwise think of. Even the spectators, wise and learned as they are, would not have come to the play if their natural hadn't drawn them into it, nor would the actors have put it on, although some of them haven't gotten their naturals straight yet because they're not used to doing it. The spectators may see a woman in the play do some things that they won't like, but since they were told about it beforehand, they must keep quiet. The narrator summarizes the plot of the play and concludes that the audience should not try to stop the characters because peasants, when they are angry, would strike the Cross. The audience must be quiet so the actors will agree to do other plays. After a few more hurried references to the plot, he departs.

The play, which Baratto has defined "a comedy of monologues,"[3] opens with the soliloquy of Menato, who swears that he is so unlucky he must have been generated when Satan combed his tail. The power of love has made him leave everything and come to Padua to follow a neighbor woman (Betia). "And he says that there's free will" (*RT,* 593). Menato is of two minds over whether to approach his erstwhile lover, finally deciding in the affirmative. Declaring his love to Betia, he urges her to run away with him. She refuses, saying that she wants to be able to look Christians in the face. If she did want to run away from her husband, she continues, she would have a better place to go, one where men are not the sons of fear, but soldiers. Menato curses his ill luck, then calms himself with the thought that Betia said she would leave Ruzante if he displeased her. Menato resolves to put him up to a trick "and she, out of spite, won't want to stay with him any longer, and I'll take her with me, and then I'll do this and that so that she'll go back to him. And then I'll be, like the guy said, the lord and master" (*RT,* 597).

Tonin, the Bergamasque soldier, enters, declaring that the military life would be a glorious one—except for the fighting—if wage months had thirty days and you could stay in your quarters and have a good time.[4] He curses the French and the Germans because he was just about to have satisfaction from a neighbor woman (Betia) when he was ordered back to the field. After an internal debate, he makes up his mind to approach her. The flirtatious conversation that ensues, reminiscent of the conventions of courtly love, concludes with a mutual declaration of willingness, but the pair is prevented from acting upon it by the return of Ruzante, who rejoices at his success in stealing some money that a soldier (Tonin) asked him to deliver.

Seeing Tonin, Ruzante reports the "theft" to him. Warming to his account, he declares that the thief looked so much like Tonin that it must have been the soldier himself, playing a trick on him. Tonin hesitates over whether to believe him, then bursts out, "By the blood of ten,[5] there never was a peasant—" Ruzante breaks in: "By the blood of the clap, we are peasants because we haven't robbed!" (*RT,* 607). Tonin announces that he doesn't want to fight and, after a few more exchanges, leaves. Exulting like Weasel (*RT,* 575) that his threats made his enemy's chin quiver, Ruzante declares, "If I put my mind to it, I'll take out three or four." (*RT,* 609). His final speech reveals that when he claims his little bit of power and money, he is no more righteous than anyone else. "I don't even want to go home. I want to go . . . I saw a girl, that I want to take out, either by force, or as the guy said . . .' [He shows the purse that he took from the soldier and exits quickly]" (*RT,* 609).[6]

Ruzante encounters Menato, who sets his plot in motion by insinuating that Betia has been unfaithful. Vehemently denying the charge, Ruzante affirms that "the benches and the chairs in the house know that when I sit down somewhere, she is already seated at my feet" (*RT,* 611). When pressed, however, he admits that lately she has been ill-tempered. Menato proposes that Ruzante learn the truth by disguising himself and offering her money, a plan the unwitting cuckold accepts.[7] They leave so that Menato may loan Ruzante a student robe. Tonin enters, amazed that for love of Betia he swallowed Ruzante's insults, but vowing to make him pay next time. The procession of soliloquys continues with Menato's jubilation over the success of his trick. He predicts that Betia will leave Ruzante and go with him because "she knows that I'm not afraid of my pal, that I make him shit bricks" (*RT,* 615). He looks for a good eavesdropping spot.

Headed for his house in student garb, Ruzante marvels at how much he looks like a Spaniard (that is, an elegant and imposing foreigner). Certain that Betia will prove her virtue, he plots to revenge himself on Menato by claiming that his student robe has been stolen by Tonin. When he arrives at the door, he realizes that he is being foolish, but decides to knock anyway. His approach to Betia is couched not in rustic dialect but in Italian (or rather *moscheto,* the kind of ungrammatical Italian attempted by dialect speakers), and sweetened with courtly words. When he offers money, Betia's worries that her husband might find out signal her willingness. Infuriated by his disgrace, Ruzante chases her into the house. He soon emerges again, this time begging her to forgive him, and swallowing whole her excuse that she had recognized him but that she was playing along as punishment. As he goes to settle his score with Menato, she slips into Tonin's house.

Ruzante's encounter with Menato repeats that of Duozo and Menego in scene 4 of the *Witty Dialogue.* Ruzante insists on how badly he was hurt and how numerous his assailants were, while Menato reiterates that he doesn't see a scratch on him. When Ruzante mentions how the "assailants" stole the student robe, though, Menato races off to reclaim it. Searching the house for Betia and desperate at not finding her, Ruzante punches and curses himself for speaking to her in Italian. He upbraids her for her lack of constancy, then begs her to tell him where she is so that they may be buried together with a long epitaph. His desolate cries prompt an old woman to lean out her window and tell him that Betia is at Tonin's house. "May the Virgin be praised, because I can still hope to enjoy her. I mustn't go acting like a bully, but be oilier than lard. If he tells me I'm a coward, I'll say that he's telling the truth. What does it matter to me, if I get what I want?" (*RT,* 627).

When he arrives at Tonin's house and asks for Betia, the soldier says that she still has to be saddled. Thinking that he is referring to a mule, Ruzante persists in his quest. Tonin maliciously continues to describe his actions as those of saddling. That Ruzante has grasped the truth of the situation is revealed in his final question: "Now would she be, like the guy said, groomed? The bride, that is" (*RT,* 629).

Betia replies from the window that she is, telling him that he has brought it on himself with his tall tales. She continues with a list of his perfidies in which the chairs play a different role. They are the place where he sits idly while she does all the work. To top it off, when they go to bed at night, he sleeps like a log. Although he attempts to return to her good graces by promising to do whatever she says, Betia withdraws. Ruzante calls Tonin to the window and asks him to put in a good word, but he refuses because of the money. Ruzante decides to commit suicide to garner Betia's sympathy. He calls out to her to have him buried and say a prayer for him. After attempting several methods, including blows to the head and self-cannibalism, he asks her to send down a rope.

Returning empty-handed, Menato urges Ruzante to seize control of the situation and get Betia back. Piqued, Ruzante tells him to do so himself since Betia is mad at him too for putting her husband up to it. Menato berates Ruzante for revealing his role to her, because it may mean they will lose her. To distract Ruzante from wondering why he should care, Menato asks if he has spoken to Tonin yet. Hearing how things are, he further berates Ruzante for getting into trouble with his tales. Ruzante slyly suggests that Menato pay the debt to Tonin since he planned the disguise.[8] Menato insists that it is Ruzante who must reclaim Betia to save his honor, but Ruzante presses him to do it for love of Betia, an argument that Menato cannot resist.

Menato promises Tonin to repay the money if he will give them their woman back, and is invited in to talk about it. Before he leaves, he attempts to impart to Ruzante the cool Boccaccian lesson that he, like Tonin, has learned: to avoid being controlled by others, you must first control yourself. "This is the way people handle things. Yeah, they don't sit around expecting manna from heaven, pal, like you do" (RT, 641). Again Ruzante follows the conversation from outside. When Menato, Tonin, and Betia emerge in agreement, Menato warns the blustering Ruzante to act like a man and not destroy his hard work.

Ruzante, unable to abide by the advice, appears at Tonin's house and tries to get "his" money back by picking a fight. Having resisted a string of verbal assaults, Tonin roars to life when his legitimacy is questioned,[9] yelling, "Shut up, you without faith, marten, swamp bird, baptized in a pig trough!" (RT, 651). Neither wants a showdown (Ruzante states in an aside that he wishes someone would come between them), so after a series of exchanges they part. When Menato returns, Ruzante, safely protected, announces his intent to fight. Menato tries to dissuade him by reminding him that the encounter may not turn out as planned and that he risks banishment from the Pavano, but Ruzante doesn't listen. Menato finally stops his friend with a plan to go armed to Tonin's house after dark and kill him.

As usual, when the moment arrives, Ruzante uses every excuse to withdraw, including the fact that he doesn't know how to run where there are walls because he's used to being out in the open. Menato finally tires of his cowardice and leaves him standing watch at the corner. Ruzante conjures up images of ghosts and monsters that become so real to him that he flees from them. Upon arriving home, he discovers that several people (Betia, Tonin, and Menato, unrecognized by him) are inside. He knocks at the door and Menato tries to get him to leave by pretending that he is someone else and yelling at Ruzante that he has the wrong house. Ruzante continues to knock; Menato comes to the door continuing his fiction and threatening Ruzante. Having earlier heard the same man beat Tonin, Ruzante drops to the ground. Betia tells Menato to go away and come back as himself to take Ruzante home.

Ruzante greets him with a tale of a horrible monster that assaulted him while he stood at the crossroads, frightening him so much that he has vowed to live in peace and even apologize to the soldier. Betia appears and begs the men to make up, pretending that it was Ruzante who beat Tonin. Willing to scavenge any glory, Ruzante imagines that he did so while running away from the monster. The play closes with Menato's proposal that they make peace and get some rest, to which Ruzante at last agrees.

Analysis. The *Moscheta* is widely recognized as Beolco's best full-length play and, together with the two *Dialogues,* the heart of his oeuvre. Situated at the transition from relative freedom to relative restraint for both Beolco and his society, it explores the complex reactions of individuals and societies to the imposition of limits. By 1530 the norms of conduct that had disintegrated in the general turmoil of the Italian Wars began to solidify around a program of piety and courtliness reflecting the coalition between Pope Clement VII and Charles V (Holy Roman Emperor and King of Spain), who, through the Peace of Bologna, became virtual rulers of Italy. The Catholic Church, whose hegemony had been compromised north of the Alps, would soon reinstitute the Inquisition to assure religious conformity where it still exercised control. The ruling classes of individual city-states, faced with decreased external political and financial opportunities, reinforced their dominance of local society as compensation.

Artists and writers soon began to incorporate the new conditions into their works, in reaction both to their culture and to their economic dependence upon patrons. Restrictions imposed by war had depleted the financial and political independence of many writers of leisured background, drawing them into the orbit of a few vastly wealthy and powerful courts, which also patronized writers of the poorer classes to insure a group of loyal publicists. The new formalism was embraced by many court writers, who became vehicles of its influence. A good example is that of Giovanni Della Casa, who, after living dissolutely as a youth, became a protegé of the papal family. He founded the Venetian office of the Inquisition (1547) and drew up a large portion of the Index of Prohibited Books, but is perhaps best known for compiling the guide to good manners which would become a byword for the genre, the *Galateo*.[10]

The position of the writers termed anticlassicists by Nino Borsellino,[11] including Beolco, was much more difficult. Prefering the spontaneity of an unregulated and unregulatable nature, they disdained the artifice made popular by the revival of classical learning, yet often depended upon the wealthy who espoused it. Common to the anticlassicists is a sense of frustration at their lack of self-determination, expressed in an oscillation between listlessness and anger. Many such writers interposed a mask between their personal and artistic identities to create a space in which to work. Frequently they became known by the corresponding nickname, as Beolco did. A similar form of disguise would be adopted by young patricians later in the century as they formed *accademie,* or social and intellectual clubs.

It is specifically this context that explains many aspects of Beolco's life and works. The question of his inheritance was not strictly one of money, rather one of personal and artistic freedom. When Beolco was not named full heir, he faced two options. He could live the life of the "shame-faced poor," a Renaissance term designating "persons of gentle birth, or at least of 'citizen' rank, who had suffered reverses of fortune which plunged them into a poverty doubly painful because they were unused to it, ashamed to beg, and ill-equipped to do manual work."[12] Such a choice would have probably involved the sacrifice of his theatrical career. The other alternative, that of finding a patron (in Beolco's case a self-congratulating pedant who took advantage of peasants' misfortunes to draw them into a regressive, semifeudal *latifondo*), allowed him to salvage it, but at considerable expense to his self-respect.

Beolco's reactions fluctuated between anger and helplessness. At times he expressed both, as in his binding of himself to Cornaro through intemperate spending. Anger gained the upper hand in *Weasel,* where he destroyed a figure resembling the man who had asked him to acquire the land of famine-stricken peasants. In the *Moscheta,* however, helplessness dominates, expressed in the philosophy that the sexual organs force human beings to act against their moral codes and commit adultery, which threatens both friendship and peaceful coexistence.

The terms of Beolco's struggle are illuminated by Elaine Pagels's recent work on Augustine of Hippo's identification of the male erection, which occurs against the consent of the individual, as the proof that there is no free will.[13] For Augustine, such lack of control, evident in other emotional and physical processes that materialize without being willed (including death), produces both internal and external conflict. The most extreme form of the latter is war, the most common, unhappiness in marriage. The resulting disorder, in his view, justified authoritarian, centralized rulership in both religious and civil spheres, as well as the use of force to maintain peace. His interpretation helped the Christian church adjust to its transformation from a persecuted minority to the state religion of the Roman Empire.

Augustine's philosophy continued to influence religious thinking through the Middle Ages, though alongside contradictory views, such as those of Aristotelian Thomas Aquinas, more at ease with the material world. They emerged as a central factor in the Reform movement of Luther, who believed that human beings were so incapable of good deeds that they could be saved only by faith.[14] Luther also supported the preservation of the social order, the responsibility for which was invested in the prince, who was entitled to use force to maintain it (though Luther was careful to hedge about the authority of princes who opposed his movement). When, in 1525, peasants inspired by his teachings and example of opposing conscience to authority rebelled against their rulers, Luther advocated a ruthless crushing of the uprising.

The change in Beolco's attitude may easily be seen in a comparison of the *Moscheta* and the *Betia,* which broach many of the same problems. In the earlier play (in which, not coincidentally, more references to Aristotle are found than in any other of Beolco's works), Nale is punished for his socially disruptive conduct by Zilio's knife wound and Tamia's hasty decision to remarry. Chastened, he acknowledges his guilt and asks both for forgiveness. Assured that Nale has understood the principle of reciprocity basic to smooth social functioning and that he will regulate his conduct accordingly in future, Zilio proposes that each man contribute his wife to a common marriage.

The *Moscheta,* instead, deals with such questions in Lutheran terms, as Mario Prosperi has noted in his analysis of Beolco's rejection of the control of passion by free will.[15] Written while Beolco was in contact with the Protestant-leaning Renée of France in Ferrara, the play shows each man to be the helpless pawn of his need for Betia. Moreover, rather than confronting his rivals to achieve exclusive possession of her, each exploits the desire of the others, forcing them to do his work for him. Thus Menato incites Ruzante to play a trick on Betia so she will leave him, Ruzante coerces Menato into paying his debt so that Tonin will return Betia, and Tonin compels Betia to induce Menato to spend the evening with Ruzante so he need fear neither, as well as playing on Ruzante's desire for Betia to insure the return of his money. Significantly, Ruzante does not defend himself against Tonin's accusation that he is without (the Catholic) faith. It is the lack of trust bred by this lack of self-control that destroys social bonds

among the characters, forcing them into isolation and generating monologues rather than dialogues.

Beolco's adaptation of scenes from contemporary plays is also instructive.
It is widely recognized that the episode in which Ruzante talks to Tonin, who
is engaged in amorous commerce with Betia (3.4), is rooted in the *Calandria*
of Bibbiena (3.10 and, I would argue, 2.10). But the surface similarity
masks profound alterations. In the *Calandria,* the man in the room is the
woman's established lover, while the one outside has only vague aspirations
to her favors. Moreover, his incomprehension of the sexual metaphor (key
and lock) seems genuine. Here, of course, the man inside the room (Tonin)
has usurped the sexual rights of the husband outside (Ruzante), whose refusal to see through the references to saddling a mule stems from his unwilling-
ness to face the consequences, namely a fight with his rival.

The play is filled with other allusions to superior, destructive forces that
impose themselves upon Ruzante or his creator. Recent critics have noted
that an important difference between the Marciana manuscript fragment
and the printed version is that the former opens with Ruzante's entrance,
delayed in the latter until scene 5. While they have interpreted the change
as expressing Beolco's artistry in heightening the audience's anticipation of
his entrance,[16] it seems to the present writer that various clues point to
another origin. That is, in *Weasel,* which immediately preceded the final
version of the *Moscheta,* a theatrical rival of Alvarotto had taken the
Ruzante-like role. It is not unlikely that Alvarotto, envious of that primacy,
insisted on being given the first entrance in the following play, as well as as-
suming himself the persona of the obsessed lover ordinarily associated with
Ruzante. Such an explanation may account for the stress the *prologista* lays
upon the primacy of the one who will come first in the play, as if to assuage
Alvarotto's jealousy. It also coordinates with the dominant role Menato
plays, in contrast with the *Betia,* where he is subdued.

Menato's new role is part of the play's emphasis on the imposition of control from outside. The ruthlessness for which he is punished in the *Betia* is
here rewarded with success. Biographical correlates again are indicative.
Menato seems to reflect the drive to control society typical of the nobility, of
which Alvarotto was a full member. That drive, which Beolco had condemned in his early career, was being forced upon him when he wrote the
Moscheta because he depended upon the patronage of Cornaro and the Este
to pursue his work.

Casting its shadow over Beolco's entire middle period is the final bodily
process, death.[17] As in other contemporary works, the protagonist attempts
to assume control over its violence by inflicting it on himself. But here the

playwright who in the *Pastoral* had scorned the epitaphs of the shepherds (and in the *Betia* had given the girl and her mother a maliciously funny one: *RT,* 403) creates a peasant who wants "a long, long epitaph that will tell of our end" (*RT,* 627). Desire for a fame that would bestow immortality may also explain Beolco's perfection of the only skill with which his contemporaries believed it would come in his profession: competence in traditional literary forms. Its first fruit is the *Moscheta*'s conformity with the classical theatrical model: five equal acts, with the most important episode, that of Ruzante's despair and Betia's infidelity, in the center; respect for the unities of time and place; and a prologue that tells the facts of the play.[18] These rules seem reified in the walls that terrify Ruzante, forced away from his home in the open country by his wife's desire for refinement.

In the *Moscheta,* anguished by his inability to change an ugly reality through passionate words, Beolco-Ruzante found his only friends among the humanized chairs and benches of a peasant house. Even their lyrical solace would be destroyed by the flaming monster who chased him from the crossroads where he stood guard into a humiliating compromise with power, a shared household resembling Cornaro's in more than passing ways. Its philosophy was best expressed in Menato's advice to Ruzante: "It's better to live a coward than die a hero" (*RT,* 655).

Flora's Play

Date and Performances. On the basis of textual reference to the famine, Emilio Lovarini dated *Flora's Play (La Fiorina)* to 1529 or 1530. Giorgio Padoan cited Sanuto's *Diaries* to support a view that the situation resembles more closely the winter of 1531–32. Like other plays of Beolco's middle years, *Flora's Play* does not exist in manuscript form. The only information about its staging occurs in a poem by the playwright's follower Gian Domenico Maganza (Magagnò), which recalls a performance in Padua.[19]

Plot and Characters. The prologue opens with an appeal to silence,[20] and continues with a condemnation of servants who speak ill of their masters. "I am a servant, but I have never taken pleasure in speaking ill of my master. And I have always done as mice do: I am happy to eat other people's food" (*RT,* 727). The wreath that the *prologista* wears on his head does not mean that he is a poet; he has been sent by the others to tell about the play, set in Jizzville in Paduan territory. They wanted him to speak in Tuscan or German or Florentine, but he didn't want to overdo. He can't understand why people do that, because keeping the natural straight delights both sexes.

Because he considers the spectators to be nothing less than brothers and sisters, the *prologista* will give them his best advice: the men should stick to the straight and narrow, and the women should let themselves be governed.[21] He goes on to praise the value of solid, moderate, peasantlike behavior in eating, drinking, and dressing (much as in the early prologues of the *Moscheta,* though with fewer double entendres). Nudity's advantage in the selection of the gender of one's partners brings some anecdotes to mind. "And if I weren't afraid that the people who sent me to recite the prologue would get mad, I'd tell you some good ones. But another time I'll pour out my heart to you" (*RT,* 731).

Neither the *prologista* nor those who sent him want any literary lions to "stick their noses" into the comedy because they want to prove that even in the countryside people find love. The *prologista* tries to summarize the facts of the plot; having mixed them up, he decides to call the actors, who will do a better job.[22] With a final admonition to the audience to keep still because the actors might get angry, he disappears.

Ruzante opens act 1 with a long soliloquy cursing himself for the mess he's in. He can't eat, drink, or sleep because he is tormented. There is no cure, because Flora, whom he loves, is cruel to him. The only relief lies in death, which, he warns the audience, should be a lesson to them to exert more self-control where love is concerned. He prays to be killed by Flora's hands, then decides to kill himself. Before doing so, he will make one more effort to pour out his heart to her.

The decision to commit suicide emboldens him to disregard the danger from Marchioro, Flora's other suitor, with whom he will have to fight to the death if the latter finds out. That image prompts him to spin a fantastic revenge. "When you've killed him, let yourself get caught, so you will die too, at the hand of justice. In this way, both of us will go to hell, and she will be the cause of this evil. And, because I've died an angry death, I will go to her in the spirit and drown her in a ditch; and what I couldn't do when I was alive, I will do when I'm dead, and get satisfaction in my own way" (*RT,* 735).[23]

Flora appears, and Ruzante addresses her with sweet words. She rejects his advances, reminding him of how he neglected her and ruined her reputation. She remains unmoved through threats of suicide, promises of pleasure, and even license to kill him if he doesn't keep his word. The possibility that the last suggestion contains a hidden mechanism of revenge against her does not escape Flora: "And what if people found out about it and they caught me and cut off my head?" (*RT,* 739). The arrival of her father Pasquale interrupts the conversation. He is going to the pasture and tells Flora to mind the house until her mother gets home.

Marchioro, who has found out about Ruzante's talk with Flora, hides near her house, vowing to trounce his rival. When, after Pasquale's departure, Ruzante attempts to resume his discussion with Flora, Marchioro jumps him. They exchange punches, then Marchioro trips his rival. Despite Ruzante's abject pleas, Marchioro beats him soundly. Returning from the fields, Pasquale breaks up the fight and asks what happened. Ruzante claims that he was just going to tend his oxen when Marchioro jumped him for no reason. Queried about why he didn't defend himself, he replies that he tripped, and that Marchioro attacked him while he was down. After the others leave, Ruzante calls himself "the unluckiest man in the whole reversal world" (*RT,* 747). If Flora saw the fight, she will know what a coward he is, so he has no recourse but to kill himself. Before he does so, however, he's going to have his injured arm looked at because he wants to die whole; "and when it's healed . . . I want to make people talk about Ruzante throughout the whole reversal world" (*RT,* 747).

Marchioro, seeing Flora leave the house to fetch water, approaches her in hopes of being praised for his valor in taking a beating (changing his role apparently to gain her sympathy). After some verbal skirmishing, they affirm their mutual desire and Marchioro proposes marriage. Flora insists that he ask her father; if he refuses, they can elope. Seeing Ruzante approach with a number of armed friends, she urges Marchioro to flee. Intending to kill his rival, Ruzante is persuaded by his companion Bedon to kidnap Flora instead so her family will accept their marriage.[24] When persuasion fails to convince her, Ruzante turns to force. Under the watchful eye of an old woman who laments the violence of modern times, the men kidnap Flora.

Returning, Marchioro is told about the episode by the old woman. Despite her assurances that Flora resisted mightily, Marchioro insists that it was a ruse, that Flora really wanted to go away with Ruzante. The woman goes to find Flora's father (Pasquale) to minimize the damage. A furious Marchioro laments the bad luck of those who trust women. He contemplates suicide, but decides to arm himself and become more famous than Magnarino, hanged for his crimes. Flora's betrayal confirms a dream he had the night before, that a sow bit his foot. After several attempts at interpretation, he settles on the oblique meaning that he will cause someone else to cease walking.

Pasquale rushes off to prevent a vendetta. Hailing Sivelo, Ruzante's father, Pasquale chides him for the conduct of his son. Sivelo confides that he has no desire to start a feud, proposing that they have Ruzante marry the girl immediately to avoid one. Praising his honorable conduct and their life-long friendship, Pasquale agrees. He further suggests that they settle the differences between the youths by giving Marchioro Ruzante's sister in marriage.

Pasquale and Sivelo call Marchioro who, after some resistance, is persuaded that his efforts to kill Ruzante may result in his own death, and that there might be someone better for him than Flora. Pasquale obtains Marchioro's authorization to act for him, adapting the standard legal and religious formulae to peasant concerns by emphasizing the erotic aspect of country life and asking for protection from the *paron*. Suspecting abuse of his permission, Marchioro warns that any bad weather will bring rain to the older man, too. The fathers agree that Marchioro will marry Sivelo's daughter; Marchioro accepts on the condition that they add her mother's skirt trimmed with silver. The bargain is sealed by Sivelo's promise to give him both the skirt and half a sow's back, from which he can make pork and cabbage (a favorite rural dish).

Analysis.   *Flora's Play* has been the subject of little critical interest because of its coldness and lack of psychological complexity.[25] Its plot is the product of too much art and too little passion and invention: each development is neatly anticipated, each character acts out a preordained role, even if it be one of anger. All loose ends are tied up at the conclusion.

Despite its neatness, however, the play does provide clues to the playwright's thinking. Sprinkled throughout are indications of Beolco's awareness that violence, which exerts a powerful influence on the plot, has serious consequences. The *prologista,* fearful that his actions will anger the other actors, curbs his tongue; the young characters commit some acts of violence but refrain from others because of their preoccupation with punishment at the hand of the law. The prologue recognizes that some servants speak ill of their masters and condemns them. This and the explicit acknowledgement that the speaker is eating food from another man's table seem to function as a public apology for the excesses of *Weasel,* particularly the murder of Andronico. Men rather than women control the love plot, as Padoan has noted, and the social disturbances created by the victory of the violent suitor are unexpectedly healed by the elders with little opposition.[26]

The violence that remains underneath, however, indicates that the new order and conservatism are merely superficial. The ending, an apparent calque of Boccaccio's parable of the victory of violent desire over civilizing love (*Decameron* 5.1, the story of Cimone), reverses Ruzante's passivity in the *Moscheta.* Beolco also inflicts violence on the more formal literary conventions that he plays upon, as they violate his earlier philosophy of the natural. Lovarini, for example, has seen in the title a satirical reference to Plautus's

Casina, in that Beolco's play "wishes explicitly to be the opposite of what those who frequent the performances of literary writers expect."[27] An even cleverer subversion, perhaps, lies behind Beolco's apparent acceptance of the Petrarchan preoccupation with love. By substituting "love" (the Petrarchan/ Bembesque byword) for "natural" in the opening discourse claiming that emotion takes away free will, he effectively turns Bembo, the aspiring cardinal, into a Lutheran. Further, the opening lines of the famous sonnet evoking Petrarch's first glimpse of Laura (*Rerum Vulgarium Fragmenta* or *Canzoniere,* 61.1–3) are recalled at the moment when Pasquale and Sivelo repair the peasant social order by promoting the erotic capabilities of an unseen girl to a youth who barters to add a skirt to her trousseau.

Violence is also evident in the relations among the members of the love triangle. The two rivals experience a hallucenatory interchange of psychological and physical harm of the other to the self, the self to the self, and the self to the other. The beloved's emotional cruelty metamorphoses into suicide, which metamorphoses into murder, which metamorphoses into execution, which metamorphoses into revenge. Moreover, Ruzante and Marchioro embrace their own executions as just retribution for the violent deeds that they fantasize, rejecting in their mental systems the moderation that such sanctions cause in their actions.

While suicide for love was a common topos of Italian Renaissance literature, it seems significant that Beolco, who had scorned it as empty puffery in the *Pastoral,* should make it a central theme in his period of greatest turmoil. His is, moreover, not a conventional pastoral treatment, but one deeply immersed in the world of folk customs and beliefs: vendettas, hauntings, spirit killings. What seems most plausible here is an interpretation close to that which Terence Murphy has given of contemporary (nonliterary) youthful suicides, where he has characterized the youth as "taking revenge upon forces beyond their control through suicide."[28] Beolco's characters, prevented by the dominant culture and perhaps by his patron from venting rage outwardly as had been done in *Weasel,* turned it on themselves in the *Witty Dialogue,* the *Moscheta,* and *Flora's Play.* The last of the three, in which the role of suicide is the most highly articulated, is also that in which conservative values are most fully accepted and thus create the greatest conflict with Beolco's enduring values.

The threat of sanctions forces Beolco here and in his remaining plays to display a surface liminal pattern accepting authority as personified in a social establishment. His rage and preferred liminoid model, however, find new (though subterranean) forms of expression, here in the victory of the violent suitor and in the last three plays in the constant criticism of aristocrats by their

servants, who dominate their betters through intelligence and resourcefulness.[29] In those plays, as servant criticism and autonomy increase, suicide
threats become confined to upperclass characters. A fully liminoid model will
return in Beolco's last work, the *Letter to Alvarotto*.

Chapter Six

"Next to the Ancients":
Masking as Plautus

The Girl from Piove and *The Cow Comedy*

Manuscripts, Date, and Performances. In December 1533, Angelo Ruzzante petitioned the Venetian Senate for the right to print two comedies, *Truffo* and *Garbinello*,[1] apparently named for the characters he played. More commonly called *The Cow Comedy (Vaccaria)* and *The Girl from Piove (Piovana)*, the comedies are adaptations of works of Plautus, the least formal of the Roman playwrights, although Beolco appears to have used Renaissance translations rather than the original Latin texts as his sources. Beolco's personal device, a medallion with the inscription "Proxime ad Antiquos" ("Next to the Ancients") over a comic mask and crossed flutes, may date to this period.

On 10 February 1532 Beolco presented a play in Ferrara, whose set had been prepared by Ludovico Ariosto; Padoan has observed that its description corresponds to *The Girl from Piove*. Paolo Sambin has found some indications that a second performance may have been staged in Padua a few days later.[2] Marin Sanudo records that during the busy Carnival season of 1533, on 17 February, a comedy by Ruzante was performed at Ca' (Palazzo) Cornaro in Padua, where, eight days later, *The Cow Comedy,* "a very beautiful new comedy" was also presented. It is commonly assumed that the unnamed comedy was *The Girl from Piove,* although Padoan proposes that it may have been the final version of the *Moscheta*. Zorzi, finding it implausible that Beolco wrote the two lengthy and diverse plays in the short time usually assigned to them, views *The Girl from Piove* as having been begun much earlier. Topics shared with *Flora's Play* and the early *Moscheta* prologues support his dating. The first act and part of the second act are found in a manuscript that also contains the *Letter to Alvarotto* and a segment of the *Canace,* a tragedy by Sperone Speroni which Beolco was preparing for the stage when he died. There are no known manuscripts of *The Cow Comedy.*

The Girl from Piove

Plot and Characters. The prologue begins with a reprise of the anti-Florentine polemic of the early *Moscheta* prologues, the speaker declaring that he refuses to change his tongue because he can express good wishes with his thick Paduan one just as well as someone else can with a fine one. He admonishes the audience to stick with the natural because it pleases both sexes. Then (like a barker at a fair or outdoor performance) he touts the virtues of the play, assuring the audience that it is new, but also that it is seasoned and sound. They may feel that they have heard it before because, as a great philosopher has told his priest, they all existed as themselves thousands of years ago, and will again thousands of years hence.[3] But that doesn't mean that anything has been stolen because the same thing has happened to the play as to some clothes found in a trunk and made over. The material is used by the living and the outdated fashion is left to the dead, so nothing is missing.[4]

The *prologista* declares that the author has used his own language, refusing exchanges and mixtures with others, because those who do that end up losing their own. All the currently popular cultural modes—lost girls, lovelorn youths, servants, gluttons, mean old men and women, ruffians—can be handled by the people of the Paduan countryside in their own language because the country existed before the city. The audience will be the judges of how the peasants succeed (a clever strategy to invoke their attention). To help them perform their task, the *prologista* tells them that behind this church near Chioggia (a fishing town on the mainland south of Venice), a fisherman caught a purse, which helped to locate a lost girl, and then there was the wedding to her beloved. Alerting them to the arrival of Siton, the beloved in search of the girl, he vanishes.

Siton enters, lamenting that a lover is like a yearling calf being teased by a cowherd who has put a thorn under his tail and a coat over his eyes. "I am the calf, love is the cowherd, the thorn is the pain that pierces my heart, and my confusion is the coat over my eyes" (*RT*, 893).[5] Nina, his beloved, has been taken from him by Slaverò, the pimp. Nearby, Daldura (a servant) calculates the damages wrought to his master's house by a storm that occurred the night before, and curses the astrologers for not foreseeing the catastrophe. Siton approaches Daldura and asks if he has seen Slaverò, explaining that he is looking for his beloved and will go to the end of the earth to find her. Daldura marvels that Siton lets himself be controlled by love instead of controlling it. Siton replies that love's decrees are imposed by force. The discussion continues, Daldura sustaining the existence of free will, Siton the imperiousness of love. Finally, vowing to destroy the pimp if he finds him, Siton enters a nearby church to search it.

Lamenting the constant sorrows of old age, Daldura's master Tura descends from the ruined roof and wonders aloud where Daldura is. Daldura thinks, "He's looking for me. But it's a pity, said Cato, if he doesn't [actually] call me, to come away from the dinner table" (*RT,* 899).[6] Eventually he answers, advising Tura to obtain construction materials from Maregale, a neighbor. Maregale in turn has his own complaints. His son (Siton) fell in love with a girl who had become separated from her family and fallen into the clutches of a pimp. The youth told his wealthy but stingy mother (Resca) of his plight. She, refusing to let him marry the courtesan, tried to force another girl upon him. The youth fled, and the pimp has taken the courtesan away. Despairing of seeing his son again, Maregale has rented some fields to get away from his odious wife. Tura advises a Stoic response: a wise man leaves the table with the same expression with which he sat down. To this, Daldura opposes his observations of real life: "Philosophy is wrong. I see crazy men and wise men that, when they have eaten and drunk well, are happier than before" (*RT,* 905).[7] When Maregale leaves, Tura admits that he was moved almost to tears by the memory of losing his only daughter in the wars.

While repairing the roof of the house, Daldura looks toward the sea and spots two girls escaping from a sinking ship. They dry off and disappear into the woods. Siton returns from his fruitless search of the church. When he hears that two girls have come ashore, he runs off, regretting only that he does not have four legs to carry him faster.

In the woods, Nina complains about the adversities of her life, that began in her childhood when she was stolen like a dog, and have persisted to recent days when she was snatched from her intended. Despite the cheery Ghetta's observation that they have at least escaped from Slaverò, Nina persists in her misery. She is happy only that the loss of her extra clothes will keep her from pleasing another man. This line of reasoning is foreign to Ghetta, who also fails to understand why Nina has chosen her man without "trying" him first, observing that some men seem virile but are worse than a woman. The two women also differ in their attitudes toward the profession that Slaverò has planned for them. Nina's preference to drown or be eaten by a wolf rather than be enjoyed by more than one husband is contradicted by Ghetta, whose hopes for happiness increase with the number of men she marries.

Their theoretical discussion is cut short by the arrival of Garbugio, Siton's servant, who thinks aloud as he walks. "The priors of the confraternity of us servants have written in the record book that there are no more than three types of masters in the world" (*RT,* 913). There are those that order the opposite of what they want, those that let you do nothing they have not ordered even though there are better ways of doing things, and those that want you to read their minds. Garbugio, however, has found a fourth type, those who want you to do a hundred things at once, like his master, whose search for his beloved requires the servants of seven estates, and who brooks no excuses.

Better bred than Nina, he greets the girls politely and insists that Nina return the courtesy despite her haste to ask about Siton. The pair tell him their story, Nina adding that she used to have tokens that would prove her identity to her father, but has lost them. Garbugio's assurance that she will find better than a father in Siton leads him to an erotic exchange with Ghetta, which he concludes by promising that he is much better than lovers who only think of how pretty their words are, then tire of the beloved.

A soliloquy by Siton reveals that his failure to find Nina has him near suicide. Meanwhile, Daldura attempts to court Ghetta, who has left the church where the girls have taken refuge. She bolts, however, when she sees Slaverò and the tavern keeper arrive. They ask Daldura about the girls, and he warns them to stay away. Later, Daldura begins to have an inkling of the girls' true identity. Noticing that they have managed to find a real bruiser (Garbugio) to protect them, he informs Slaverò and the tavern keeper of their location in the hope that Garbugio will fight them off. When Garbugio is approached by the pair of ruffians, he at first threatens them, then appears to give up. They rush the church, where he has had the girls tear down all the statues of the saints, and he closes them inside. He then cries for help; Tura responds and Garbugio tells him that the destruction has been caused by two Lutherans.[8] Tura calls the local men, who beat the "infidels" soundly.

Tura entrusts the girls to his neighbor Maregale while Garbugio goes to find his master. Siton, meanwhile, having found that love is a fire that can be put out only by the money that eludes him, wanders even closer to the brink of suicide. Unbeknownst to him, Maregale has discovered that Nina is his beloved, and his servant Garbinello has concocted a plan to wheedle money for the girl's dowry out of the stingy Resca. Unfortunately the plan has failed, leaving Garbinello worried that he will be disowned by his family, which vaunts its ability to weave deceptions. His scheme was to convince the old woman that Siton had been caught in the house of a merchant's daughter and, to avoid dishonoring himself by a lowly marriage, was required to pay her fifty lira for a dowry so that she might marry someone else.[9] But Resca would not listen to him. Garbinello is in the midst of cooking up a better story when he is stopped by the sight of his mistress.

Less hard-hearted than she seems, Resca has brought the money and is searching for her son. Unaware of her intent, Garbinello approaches and begins to weave his new tale, informing her that her husband has disgraced her by taking two extra wives. Infuriated, Resca gives the money to Garbinello, and leaves to reclaim her dowry and separate from her husband. Upon arriving home, she chases the two girls from the house. Maregale denies the charges, but his efforts are complicated by the arrival of a fisherman, to whom Maregale had (jokingly?) explained that the young women were his girlfriends. The (deliberately?) dense fisherman repeats all the nasty things Maregale had said about Resca in their earlier conversation, until Maregale finally indicates that she is the woman present. Garbinello, meanwhile, after keeping Siton in suspense about whether he has obtained the money or not, finally reveals that both it and the girl are at hand.

In the meantime, Bertevello, one of Tura's servants, has gone fishing and found a rich purse. He plans to tell his master that he no longer wants to live with other people, then to go off and buy farms and lands and build houses and have children that will bear his name. He will sleep and order servants about and have enough to eat, and maybe even be called "Sir." Everyone will talk about him. His dream is interrupted by Garbugio, who saw him catch the purse-fish, and wants half. Bertevello argues that anything taken from the sea is common property, but Garbugio asserts that that principle applies only to what is born in the sea. The quarrel degenerates into a tug-of-war over the purse. Nina and Ghetta arrive with Tura; discovering that tokens found inside the purse prove that Nina is his daughter, Tura confiscates it. Furious at his loss and his carelessness, Bertevello decides to commit suicide.

Attempting to placate Resca and find a way for the girls to stay in his master's house, Garbinello tries to convince Resca that Nina is the sole heir of a rich man (an unwitting truth) and should be courted. Resca's greed is piqued, and Garbinello urges her to return to Nina's good graces by welcoming her as the daughter she lost in the wars. Meanwhile, Garbugio reminds Tura that he has done his duty as a servant and that Tura must keep his word and persuade Siton to let him have the use of a farm and give him Ghetta as his wife. Tura agrees, even promising to provide her with a dowry.

Bertevello, particularly irate that the servant who spied on him will marry Ghetta as compensation, decides to advertise the finding of the purse and obtain a reward. He first plans to fulfill his dreams with the reward money, but as his fury mounts he renews his vow to commit suicide so no one will ever take anything from him again. Garbinello, feeling deserted as Siton dedicates all of his energies to Nina, consoles himself with the thought of the food he will eat at the wedding banquet, filling out his stomach after years of famine. He marvels at Garbugio's foolhardy desire to marry and spoil the pleasures of eating with a shrewish wife. His wish, on the other hand, is not to be given

commands during the days of the feast, but to be allowed to lie around and
enjoy himself.

Bertevello's advertisement attracts Slaverò and the tavern keeper, reunited
by their plans to trick him and keep the purse. Garbinello and Daldura
(planning to keep the purse themselves) scare them off with a warning that
Nina's newly found father will lead a family vendetta against them.
Bertevello, meanwhile, presses his claim with Tura, who rejects it on the
grounds that his conscience dictates restoration of found goods to the owner.
They encounter the other servants, and the three claimants begin to quarrel.

> *Bertevello:* What right do you have?
>
> *Garbinello:* We have fallen heir to it.
>
> *Bertevello:* There are closer and more direct heirs than you,
> and yet they can't have it (*RT,* 1033).

Garbinello and Daldura finally convince Tura that Slaverò left them the
purse to pay for religious services for his soul as he was being carried off by the
Venetian police. The play closes with Tura's instructions that they divide it in
three, and with Bertevello's curse.[10] Garbinello turns to the audience and
urges them to shout and frighten the pimp away.

Analysis.   Some critics hold that Beolco turned to ancient sources because he had exhausted the resources of the *mariazo* and dialogue forms, or
because he wished to continue his pursuit of high culture. Nino Borsellino
and Mario Baratto, however, view Beolco's use of Plautus as the new basis for
a dialect alternative, Baratto in particular noting the ways in which Beolco re-
cast the Plautine text in contemporary terms, prizing realism over adherence
to the source.[11] Their explanation correlates with other evidence pointing to a
revival of Beolco's polemic in his late phase, particularly the liminoid social
reality beneath the play's liminal surface (the servants save the girls and
trounce the bullies, a servant fisherman finds the purse proving Nina's high
birth, Maregale is ruled by his rich wife, etc.) and the return of Aristotle as archetypal sage. A further reason for Beolco's use of ancient prototypes may
have been his sensitivity to the Renaissance search for immortality through
literary fame, a fame that could be attained only through (apparent) adherence to mainstream genres.

In adopting the two-tiered society of masters and servants of the Plautine
plays, Beolco stabilized the opposition between passivity and aggression that
had alternated in his middle period like the ends of a seesaw. While superfi-
cially acknowledging the established power and wealth of the former, he

demonstrated their dependence upon the superior industry and resourcefulness of the latter. The duality extends to the two roles played by Beolco, servants Garbinello and Garbugio.[12] Garbugio, forthright and awkward, performs the heavy work of the play. He is rewarded with the farm and wife that will satisfy his need to perpetuate himself, a drive echoed by Bertevello. He is then eclipsed by his more sophisticated double when the wealthy Resca enters the play. All is not well with Garbinello, however. His cleverness and polish, while admirable by the standards of high culture, are byproducts of a sterility wrought of hardship that depletes him of all desires except those for food and rest. Descended from the Ruzante who felt powerless to cope with women, Garbinello renounces them entirely.

The aspect of the play that has attracted most critical attention is its derivation from the *Rudens* or *Rope* of Plautus, augmented by contributions from other ancient sources. Some material is also furnished by Renaissance plays, particularly Ariosto's *Cassaria* (also an adaptation of the *Rudens*) and the *Stephanium* of Giovanni Antonio Marso (a member of the Crociferi), performed in Venice earlier in the century.[13] Work on the more significant question of how Beolco adapted the sources to his own concerns was begun by Grabher in his insightful observations on Beolco's infusion of humor, lyrical vitality, and Goldoniesque sentimentality in the Plautine text.

Reworkings include adjustments of names and places to ones of local interest. The coast of Africa becomes the fishing port of Chioggia south of Venice, where many peasants fled during the wars. The church, inspired by an apparition that occurred while Cornaro's uncle held the canonicate there, was completed in 1529. Tura, from Ventura or Bonaventura, was a common given name in the area, and that of a notary in Este before whom Beolco had testified. Piove was the center of the region where Beolco had been acting as Cornaro's agent.[14]

More importantly, the playwright altered source materials to bolster his own polemic, or to explore subjects of concern. The episode of Bertevello, for example, was expanded from the five scenes of the Plautine play to nine. The other servants were added, creating the problem of dividing spoils among equals with competing rights. It does not seem accidental, in light of Beolco's own inheritance problems, that he added the terminology of inheritance and Bertevello's sense of his greater natural right being overturned by force and trickery (*RT,* 1011).

A further example of adaptation is found in Nina and Ghetta's discussion of men and love, which transforms the Plautine original, where both girls threaten to commit suicide rather than stay with the pimp, into a class-based debate on mores. Nina, an aristocrat, adheres to her class's norm of chastity, a restraint that correlates with the perpetuation of privileges through a limited birth line. Ghetta argues for the values of the working class, where women are freed from such restraints by their own work and by the lack of goods to transmit. It is she, whose philosophy corresponds with the probable conduct of Maria, Beolco's putative mother, who has the last word. Into this context Beolco introduced a passage adapted from the *Decameron* 5.3 (that it is better to be torn apart by men than to be ripped to shreds by wild beasts). The heroine of the Boccaccian tale, wandering in the woods, faces the genuine risk of being eaten alive if she spends the night outdoors. When she discovers the hut of an elderly couple, she finds their warning that they might not be able to protect her from marauding brigands the lesser of two evils. Nina and Ghetta, on the other hand, in no immediate danger, express absolute preferences.[15]

Nor does the play espouse the high-culture view that aristocrats are superior to the poor. When the two groups are juxtaposed, it is more often the former who lose. Disabled by their preoccupation with high ideals, they whine about their troubles, unlike the peasant-servants who find practical solutions. It is the masters' heavy demands and lack of consideration that cause the servants to lie. Nina's abandonment of common courtesy in the name of love, for example, prompts Garbugio to lecture her on manners. Such evidence signals the dangers of interpreting Beolco's turn to regular comedy as unqualified acceptance of its authority.

Beolco's true authorization, embodying a liminoid philosophy, comes from the empowerment of the lowly. He cites peasant proverbs and oracular figures in the Plautine plays far more frequently than in earlier ones, and by archetypal peasant names rather than such formulae as "the guy who." Self-authorization for peasant social institutions is found in the stress given by Garbinello to his ancestors, and by Bertevello to his founding of a house and village. Moreover, Garbugio creates a confraternity of servants (the equivalent of a union) with its own charter, in which they empower themselves to judge their social superiors. Such a move was unheard of in Renaissance Italy, where only certain independent trades were permitted to incorporate and servants were under the authority of their masters.

Of equal importance are those subjects upon which Beolco seems to dwell out of personal interest: old age and impending death, which impel a man to immortalize himself; Garbinello's retreat from powerless relationships with women into the certain pleasures of food; the domination of apparently lower-class Maregale by a stingy, rich wife; the servants' loss of identity in the face of their masters' incessant demands; the spinning of elaborate falsehoods to defend oneself against the powerful; the pitting of the poor against one another; and the restrictions on material resources that lead even the rich to count such minor household items as buckets. These come from a man approaching forty, constrained to fight for a fraction of a patrimony so shrunken that his cousins would soon quarrel about buying clogs for his half sisters, possibly ill with malaria, the right hand and virtual servant of a perpetually busy landowner and church administrator, married but probably living apart from a well-dowered wife, a childless writer-actor contemplating impressing his performances upon the immortal page.

The Cow Comedy

Plot and Characters. In accord with ancient practice, *The Cow Comedy* has two prologues. The first is recited by an elf, Beolco's reinterpretation in folk terms of the traditional Mercury (messenger of the gods and the underworld). Plautus, he says, has sent him to tell the audience not to curse the comedy if it is not in Latin, or in verse,[16] or in any way refined, because if he were alive today, he would write his comedies in just this way. Moreover, the audience is not to compare it with the written form of Plautus' plays "because many things that work on the page flop on the stage" (*RT,* 1043).

The second prologue is more typical Beolchian fare, developing some of the sexual themes of the prologues of the *Moscheta* and *Flora's Play*. The peasant speaker (Truffo) announces that he has been sent because the elf stole the voice of the person who was supposed to come.[17] Though he is not very confident of his abilities, he at least won't overdo but will stick to the natural, instead of going on the wrong side or putting things that belong on the bottom on top.

He of course is not referring to the women who are high above everyone else (on risers) because they are angels. In fact, they are protected by all kinds of uprights—thick, short, long—from falling to the ground. The good man who organized the party had the risers built so the women could take full pleasure in the show. There is no place for pleasure where there is worry. Thus if the members of the audience have debts, they should let the person to whom they owe the money worry about it. If they want to become rich, they should run to Count Pandin who will give them loads of gold. If they are unhappily married, they should forget about it because only one man is happy with his wife.[18] Such worries keep pleasure from entering into the head; finding his way blocked, he will spill over outside, and the audience will be at fault.[19] He has a special solution for women whose husbands desert them for another: he will give them a little *animalet* to attach to their waists instead of those baubles they wear, and when their husbands go away, he will take them and restore them with that.[20]

Realizing that he has strayed from his subject, the speaker returns to his job of introducing the comedy, which is not of asses, as in days of old (a reference to the *Asinaria* or *Comedy of Asses* of Plautus, on which it is based), because if they were to come up on the risers they would bray and fart. Instead it is about cows, much more useful and pleasure-giving animals, and thus always to be found about the house.[21] The play is set in Padua; the audience will understand from the speaker and his old master that the latter's son (Flavio) is in love with a courtesan (Fiorinetta), daughter of a madam (Celega). Having run out of money, he is about to lose access to her. Thus his father (Placido) and the servant (Truffo) wish to find him money on their own.

The first act opens with a dialogue between Truffo and Placido on the importance of a father's pleasing his son, even to the extent of procuring a prostitute for him. Borrowing a metaphor from the *Second Oration,* Beolco compares a father and son's love for each other with a rope, each end of which must be pulled with equal vigor, or one of the pullers will end up with his ass on the ground (*RT,* 1051). Truffo suggests that Placido meet his son's needs by arranging a marriage, but the master's own bad marriage makes him hesitate. Truffo says that wives should be like horses, returnable within a certain time if defects are found. Country people, he assures Placido, rarely make such mistakes because they get to know the woman well first; "but you, as long as you increase your wealth, don't care about anything else" (*RT,* 1054). The two elaborate on the unpleasant qualities of Placido's rich, stingy wife Rospina, whom he avoids angering for fear that she will give her dowry to priests and friars rather than to their son, who will perpetuate the life of the father in his descendants.

Placido finally admits that Flavio needs money to retain his right to Fiorinetta, and orders Truffo and fellow servant Vezzo to procure it. Truffo despairs until Placido authorizes him to use trickery if need be. Confident that his servant would die rather than fail at a task, he departs for a relaxing shave. The preoccupied Truffo seeks the companionship of stories and fables, comforting himself with the knowledge that "I am worth something because, if he hadn't known I was good, he wouldn't have told me to do it" (*RT,* 1059).

The scene changes to Flavio's excoriation of Celega for her greed, which, in his opinion, will bring about the ruin of her daughter. The madam counters by accusing him of arrogantly using his high social position to obtain favors for nothing. She defends her conduct as necessary for earning her bread, rejecting his proposal to defer payment until his mother dies because she must pay the tradesmen now. Her boast that another customer, Polidoro, will pay immediately sends Flavio off to the moneylender.

In the meantime, Truffo brags that to be a good servant one has to be bad, a qualification he possess in full. Vezzo joins him, and they criticize city people for being incapable of dealing with any problem that does not have a solution written in a book, thinking wistfully how wise peasants would seem if they had all the money. Truffo asserts, "Let these rich people do what they want because they can't do without us anyway. If we weren't servants, they wouldn't be masters" (*RT,* 1071).[22] Vezzo proposes that they set the old woman's house on fire and, while everyone is fleeing, grab the strongbox and push her in the fire. But, partly to avoid the punishment for such a deed, they will then throw water on the fire and rescue her.[23]

Truffo's solution is less dangerous. Having heard that a merchant was seeking their master's steward to pay for some cows, Truffo told him to look for a man resembling Vezzo. The merchant and the disguised Vezzo are engaged in conversation when the real steward arrives, lamenting the difficulties of working in families where the master has died and left the steward to fulfill his duties over the self-indulgence of family members.[24] Truffo distracts him with a speech on the unique ability of pleasure to multiply when it is divided among several people, asserting that laughter is better than bread because it lengthens life. He launches into a complex tale of a trickster and succeeds in duping the steward into giving him some money.

Meanwhile, Celega attempts to convince Fiorinetta that admitting Flavio to her house without exacting payment will be her financial ruin, and that she should accept the well-heeled Polidoro.[25] Fiorinetta, affirming the importance of love, rejects Polidoro because he is ugly and infected with syphilis. Exasperated, Celega appeals to Fiorinetta's desire to become wealthy; the shrewd way is to show everyone the rich presents given to her by her clients, inducing them to compete. Nina, who has done so, has gone from frequenting taverns to dressing in silk and commanding servants. Undetered, Fiorinetta asserts her preference for marriage, which Celega denigrates as placing the woman under the will of a man.

Truffo and Vezzo rehash with relish the trick they played on the merchant to obtain the money for Flavio. They compare favorably their roles as servants to those in learned comedies put on in the Palace at Carnival, affirming the superiority of country people over city people. Truffo praises his old master for playing along, predicting that he will take a share of Fiorinetta's favors.

The young lovers appear and, in a long duet, decide to commit suicide, Fiorinetta to revenge herself upon her mother. The servants, watching the lovers unobserved, comment upon the vacuousness of such promises, though Truffo admits that sometime lovers accidentally succeed. They decide to pro-long the couple's agony by delaying the revelation that the money has been obtained. Flavio sighs that he would die willingly if he could add his remain-ing life to Fiorinetta's. They kiss, and Fiorinetta, overcome with emotion, faints. Vezzo suggests that they revive her by peeing in her face, since they have no rose water. When she does not respond to Flavio's entreaties, he and Truffo fear that she is really dying, and rush to help. As they assure Flavio that they have the money, she revives.

Before giving the sum to Flavio, however, Truffo wants assurances that "if this were discovered, it should not appear that I or any of my ancestors could have done it" (*RT*, 1113). The hint that the money's origin is not honorable leads Flavio to discover, to his astonishment, that it did not come from his fa-ther. Truffo dryly replies that the father never has had any, and that the money is buried treasure brought by a magician. To prolong the suspense, Truffo spins a long tale about posing as a groom and escaping with the dowry money,[26] which he now has for Flavio. But before giving it to him, Truffo wants assurances that he will not suffer any legal consequences for the way in which he obtained it. Flavio's promise that he personally will make restitu-tion is received with the same skepticism that greeted his promise of deferred payment, because Truffo knows that he is an unemancipated son.[27] Vezzo fi-nally promises that if Truffo is caught, he (Vezzo) will claim that he commit-ted the crime. The pair will then tell so many confusing stories that they will be let go for lack of evidence. Celega is called to receive her payment, and Truffo announces that Placido is preparing a feast.

Loron, a self-flattering sycophant who frequents Polidoro,[28] encounters Truffo, who gives him a verbal drubbing for acting the buffoon instead of working. Loron retorts that, unlike buffoons, who always stand because they are busy entertaining the diners, he is the first to be seated. Moreover, buf-foons make other people laugh, while he laughs at others. Truffo gets even with Loron for his condescension by revealing that he and Flavio have won the competition for Fiorinetta.

Meanwhile, an unwitting Polidoro visits the notary to have a detailed con-tract drawn up forbidding Fiorinetta contact with any other man during his year of possession, and guaranteeing replacement days for any missed.[29] Loron encounters him just as he has learned the unpleasant truth and offers a plan of revenge: he will inform Rospina that both father and son are engaged in illicit pleasures.

The scene shifts to Vezzo's courtship of Celega's maid, Betia, who demurs, like her namesake in the *Moscheta* when approached by Tonin, saying that her beauty is not half what it was in the country. She counters his invitation to join him with an affirmation that she cannot leave a mistress who is good to her. Vezzo bitterly tries to disabuse her of this notion, asserting that masters work their servants hard as long as they are strong, then discard them.

Placido and Flavio approach Celega's house for the feast, the father proposing to take Fiorinetta for that night. As he promises her one of Rospina's richest skirts, the latter arrives with Loron. Rospina now reinterprets his frequent dining away from home and the disappearance of her household items as products of similar behavior. But it is when he describes in humiliating detail his revulsion for her that she bursts in, filled with indignation.

In a surprise conclusion, Rospina converts (offstage and between acts) because of the experience of hearing what people really think of her.[30] Truffo explains her change of heart with an odd image of life as a stalk that has good and bad placed along it like leaves, so that (like an insect?) one gets to the base of one and commences along the next. Celega tells Rospina that she too has been inspired to change her life. Celega attempts to justify her present work by stating that she took it up "not to become rich but to flee poverty," and that Fiorinetta came to her by chance. She became much more intent upon pursuing money, she says, once she became aware of "the scant respect that the great and powerful show for the poor" (*RT,* 1159). Underneath, however, she still harbors good intentions. Prefiguring the chaste prostitute of later plays, she declares that if it hadn't been for the promise that she had made to someone to raise Fiorinetta, she would have entered the Convent of the Repentants ten years earlier.[31] She had hoped that Flavio would do the honorable thing in Fiorinetta's regard. Equivocating, Rospina says that if he has done anything unworthy he will make amends, but cautions that those who assent to bad deeds are sometimes worse than those who commit them. Her good will toward Vezzo restored, Rospina promises him Betia's hand in marriage (aided by a dowry) and the use of a farm.

Fearing that Flavio will be in danger if he goes to Fiorinetta's house during Carnival, Rospina proposes that the young woman stay with them during that unruly season. Her revenge upon her husband is mild: she teases him by making him believe that Flavio and Fiorinetta will marry that very day. Her discovery that he opposes the union because of the girl's low social status apparently motivates her to turn the joke into reality.

Vezzo, aglow at the thought of marrying and going off on his own, urges Truffo to do the same. His friend, though, prefers to leave the risk-taking to their master. Both approve of Rospina's change of heart, believing that it has come from her fear of them, and agreeing that all women should be subjugated that way. The singer Piolo, hired to entertain at the wedding feast, joins them, proclaiming that he has learned from the magpies to sing for his supper. The three trade insults and anticipate the pleasure of consuming the feast being prepared. Piolo warns the others not to eat from his plate because the last fellow who tried it lost two teeth and his supper when Piolo made the buckle fly off his belt and hit him in the face. The play trickles off in a rehearsal of popular songs in preparation for the wedding.

Analysis. In *The Cow Comedy,* as in *The Girl from Piove,* Beolco uses a liminal surface to mask a functionally liminoid society ruled by youth, servants, and women. The plot is set in motion by Flavio's love for Fiorinetta; Placido, abdicating authority over his son, submits to the youth's desires. The money needed to obtain Fiorinetta is exacted by a woman and procured by servants from another woman, whose large dowry empowers her to fill most of the functions previously assigned to patriarchs.[32] Rospina purchases the cows, invites her son to bring Fiorinetta into the house against the father's will, and settles the farm and the dowry upon Vezzo and Betia. The minor concession that she makes to traditional notions of female occupations in 5.3 comes, significantly, only after she has performed these actions (*RT,* 1159).

Beolco depicts the upper class's claims to refinement and their relegation of vulgar chores to servants as a cover for their inability to deal with life, as well as veils concealing the ugly truth that, lacking in ideals, they are obsessed with position and money. Characters of high social status, first given an important role in *The Girl from Piove,* are identified linguistically in *The Cow Comedy* by their use of Tuscan. They include not only Flavio, Placido, Rospina, and Polidoro, but also Celega, Fiorinetta, the merchant, and the steward. The assemblage appears to be an odd one until one realizes that it consists of the characters unable to distinguish between words and reality (see 2.5, especially paragraph 158), or who live in a world of rhetoric that allows them to exploit (or cooperate in the exploitation of) the powerless. Even the unsavory Polidoro appeals to the Tuscan speakers because of his money and patina of culture.

The real protagonists are those whose resourcefulness and latitude of conduct enable the self-styled idealists to achieve their goals: Truffo and Vezzo. They, along with Betia, Loron, and Piolo, real people with genuine emotions, are the speakers of Paduan country dialect. As Grabher noted, the vitality of the servants, their enduring connection to the countryside, and their appreciation of their own capabilities are peculiarly Beolchian,[33] not found in the source material. While these characters accede to the requirements of power and money, they have the honesty to admit that their work is repellent and dictated by the need to survive. Piolo, for example, compares himself to a dog that has been domesticated to assure himself food (*RT,* 1171), and Loron admits to laughing at those off whom he lives.

Truffo here is an ambiguous figure, at first unwilling to pursue money, yet later boasting about his ability to obtain it through trickery. He is capable of recognizing the repulsiveness of Loron's situation, yet unable to face the sycophant's hints that they exercise the same craft. He criticizes masters, yet is unwilling to leave their service for the risk-filled life of marriage and farming. Truffo's struggle seems to parallel Beolco's own conflicting attractions to the hypocritical but secure and pleasant life of the powerful, on the one hand, and, on the other, the honest but uncertain existence of the humble, often subject to outside control and depredation.

The additions that the playwright incorporated into the translation reveal much about his concerns, in particular a troubled awareness of hardening social distinctions based on money, a commodity grown scarce in a society torn apart by a generation of expensive and economically disruptive wars. To Flavio and Celega's exchange (1.4) have been added Flavio's threat to make Celega earn her bread, his impatient awaiting of his mother's death, and Celega's vilification of the rich. Both characters attempt to serve their own interests, Celega by forcing Flavio to pay rather than expect unearned privileges, and he by lording his superior social status over her. Truffo's two soliloquys on his happiness at his task of finding money (1.2, 4.1) and his duet of coin names with Vezzo (2.1) have also been added, indicating that the masters' anxieties have become the labor of the servants.

While the wealthy and powerful still maintain their overt control, in the play as well as in history, the humble win the moral victory of being recognized as the mechanism upon which society depends. Their power, which must remain concealed in the official world, is exercised in the liminic[34] sphere of pleasures and invention (tales, play, song, and food) with which the comedy concludes.

Chapter Seven

Ruzante's Farewell

The Woman from Ancona

Manuscripts, Date, and Performances. *The Woman from Ancona (L'Anconitana)* exists in two manuscript copies, one in the Marciana miscellany, the other in the Verona City Library; it was also included in early printings.[1] While there are no sure attestations of performances, the playwright apparently expected one in Padua and one in Venice, since the apostrophe of the four lovers appears in forms suited to each city.

The play's date is one of the most vexed questions of Beolco studies.[2] Alfred Mortier, on the basis of a rather general description of Beolco's career by Aldus Manutius's son, hypothesized a date of 1529–32, accepted by Lovarini. The play would thus mediate between the early peasant works and the later Plautine ones. Zorzi, however, was induced to assign the play a date of 1522 because of his sense of the playwright's evolution, the play's resemblances to the *Betia* and the *First Oration,* and internal references to the Turkish threat.

Opposition to such an early date was expressed by Grabher, who stressed the maturity and sentimentalism of the work and the constancy of the perception of Turkish threat during the entire period but especially in 1537 and 1538. Nino Borsellino defended Zorzi's date, emphasizing the play's similarity to the *Pastoral,* the youth of its protagonist, its lack of polemic for the natural, links with the *Calandria* staged in Venice in 1522, and the contemporary quality of the reference to Cyprus. Such a dating for Borsellino was linked with Beolco's gradual discarding of theatrical tradition as he progressed in his exploration of the peasant world. In his complete edition of the works, Zorzi compromised, placing *The Woman from Ancona* directly before the two Plautine plays but affirming in the notes his conviction that it had been written much earlier.

A further revision has been proposed by Padoan. Citing renewed Turkish aggression between 1532 and 1534, he assigned the play to the latter part of that period, adducing as further proof its acceptance of the previously scandalous fashion of pierced ears, its regular structure, the large number of characters, the urban setting, and the greater shrewdness of Ruzante as servant. Borsellino wrote again to oppose a late date and the value given it by Padoan, that is, Beolco's rejection of his earlier polemic in favor of a more conventional literary stance. Borsellino noted that the considerable recognition given Beolco for his peasant works would argue against a late change in style, and opposed Padoan's apparent method of constructing a theory prior to searching for data. He also found the historical details adduced by Padoan less than convincing. He noted that earrings, for example, adorn the patrician ladies of a Venetian painting of about 1500, and occur in other literary works of the late fifteenth and early sixteenth centuries. He observed the play's closeness to the *Pastoral* in the isolation of Ruzante and noted the large number of actors in the *Pastoral* and the *Betia*. Finally, Borsellino characterized the Plautine plays as a new instrument chosen by Beolco to address the opposing forces of his dramatic work, one that the playwright was unlikely to have discarded for the experimentalism of *The Woman from Ancona*.

Each group of scholars presents evidence for which the other dating scheme cannot account, and more material may be added on both sides of the question. For example, the clothes that Ruzante plans to buy (parti-colored pants, jacket, red hat, feather) are much closer to the fashions of young patricians and their servants early in Beolco's career than those of the date proposed by Padoan. In Venetian paintings of that period, patrician youths usually display two or three of the four components, while all four occur in the dress of their gondoliers. Later fashions were more sober, chiefly black and white, and less revealing in cut.[3] As in the early plays, the theme of natural abundance occurs in *The Woman from Ancona,* but the cameo appearance of Menato, who after the *Moscheta* virtually disappears from Beolco's works, supports the hypothesis that the play was rewritten late in Beolco's career. In particular, the symmetry that a full role for Menato would give the play hints that his part had been reduced: with the servant Ghitta as his sweetheart, there would have been two pairs of peasant lovers (as in the *Betia*), paralleling the two pairs of refined lovers. The above evidence persuades the present writer that *The Woman from Ancona* is an early play rewritten at the end of Beolco's career, perhaps in response to pressures for material or perhaps as a summary of his work.[4] Such a position, however, accompanies a critical interpretation sympathetic to that of Borsellino, as will be seen below.

Plot and Characters. Like *The Cow Comedy, The Woman from Ancona* is introduced by a prologue in Tuscan and one in Paduan. Time, who delivers the Tuscan prologue, promises that, though he cannot stop the movement of the hours, he will not let them count toward the length of the audience's lives. The second section gives the longest plot summary of any of the prologues, stressing the play's concern with a novel case of love that will bring the audience pleasure. It concerns three youths who were enslaved by pirates, sold to a Moor, and ransomed by a Venetian merchant.

The Paduan prologue declares that, because of the intrigues of the world, some men like to go with animals and become herdsmen, some like to keep the house in order, some to make money, some to fight. Some, having been struck with the arrows of Love, think of nothing else. In fact, that is what has happened in Padua, where a beautiful love story took place. Since Love (Cupid) and his mother (Venus) fled their home in Cyprus for fear of the Turks, they have taken refuge inside the strong walls of Padua, causing everyone to fall in love. Love affects the animals and plants, making them reproduce and alleviate human hunger. Moreover, love is of service to human beings, for, without love, husband and wife might be of different desires, but love jumps in between them and helps us all be conceived.[5] For love of those men of letters who say that making comedies means eating, there will be two comedies.[6]

The *prologista* exhorts the women in the audience to welcome love. He can attest to its good effects, because once he didn't believe in love and tried to get rid of it. When it started moving around, he took his tool in hand and shoveled and hoed so hard that poor love lowered its head and slipped away. Having tried love, the *prologista* now knows how much pleasure it brings. Concluding with the vague and garbled account of the plot that characterizes the peasant-delivered prologues, he withdraws.

Three youths appear on stage speaking in Tuscan, one (Tancredi) declaring that he sees no other way for them to free themselves but to rely on their skills in making women beautiful. Some gentlewoman will wish to acquire such knowledge and repay the merchant the ransom that he paid to the Moor. They will then serve her until money arrives from their homeland of Sicily. If that does not happen, servitude to a gentlewoman would be preferable to freedom. Teodoro agrees.

Tancredi, told by Gismondo to greet a gentlewoman (Doralice, actually a courtesan) who has appeared at her window,[7] explains their plight to her. He describes his particular art, poetry whose praise of a woman's beauty is so exquisite that it makes her universally and eternally appealing. Teodoro's specialty is the compounding of pure, natural cosmetics and perfumes that will make a woman enticing without leaving unappealing dregs.[8] Gismondo explains that, fleeing the wrath of his relatives as a youth, he disguised himself as a woman and learned needlework in a convent. Thus he is capable of embroidering lifelike scenes on cloth, and dressing ladies in refined clothing and accessories that will best bring out their beauty. Doralice acknowledges the importance of their work, defending women's love of cosmetics with their need to keep their husbands from other women. Recalling how Petrarch immortalized Laura, she acknowledges her interest in their services, but admits that she has no money with which to hire them. She encourages them to seek other Paduan women, famous for their generosity.

Meanwhile Tomao, a Venetian broker like Cornaro and Andronico, grumbles about the failure of his efforts to achieve peace with his wife by coming to Padua for a change of air. She's always asking to spend his money to satisfy her appetites, even requesting recently that he buy a slave of the Turks for a servant. Tomao admits that the slave (Gismondo) can sew, and hopes that the youth can serve both his wife and him. In fact, the youth may even distract his wife enough for him to pursue the beautiful foreign woman he's enamoured of (Doralice). The old man sets off to look for his servant Ruzante, who has not yet returned from running an errand.

On his way about town, the Paduan-speaking Ruzante complains about the new servant. Making fun of the artificial refinement of his language and speculating on the real work his mistress wants the new man to do with his needle, Ruzante wonders why his master has not yet perceived the danger. Remembering that Tomao too is in love, he exclaims over the blindness it produces. There are three loves attached to a single stalk:[9] his master is in love with Doralice, he with her maid, and his mistress with the prisoner of the Turks. "By the clap, this is really a beautiful story! God help me, I think I've figured it out better than any of them" (*RT,* 803). He stops at Doralice's house to court Bessa, the peasant maid. She tells him that he can show his affection by convincing his master to pay a certain debt of Doralice's. Then, she promises an ecstatic Ruzante, the four of them can go out to the country together.

Ruzante, arriving home, hears that Gismondo is actually a woman. He leaves the house laughing that the "great story" (*RT,* 811) and encounters Tomao. Telling him what a bad animal-buyer he would make, Ruzante recounts the news, saying that the screaming of the two desperate women has driven him out of the house. Though Tomao claims that he had already had his doubts, a stray remark reveals that he in fact had not suspected. Eventually he asks about Doralice, only to hear a lengthy account from Ruzante of how Bessa loves him. Ruzante also draws him into a singing contest in which the servant reveals his hostility toward his master through such (invented?) popular song lyrics as "I would like to see your heart cut out" and "A knife through your chest in the middle of your heart" (*RT,* 815).[10]

Amused at his performance, Tomao observes, "You must be called Buzzer (Ruzante) because you're always buzzing." In response, Ruzante gives the famous explanation of his name: "My right name is Perduoçimo.[11] Now when I was growing up and going around with the animals, I was always buzzing, with mares or cows or sows or ewes. And then I had a dog, that I had raised for myself, that I had trained to be led around by the hand, so that you would have said, 'It's a donkey.' I was always buzzing with him; I would spit in his face so I could get him aside and go behind some big bush and buzz with him. And that's why they call me Buzzer, because I used to buzz" (*RT,* 817).

Tomao asks how things are going with Doralice. Ruzante says that someone has been saying nasty things to her about Tomao, how old he is, how he stinks and has hemorrhoids, that he looks like a scarecrow. Incensed, Tomao strips to his shirtsleeves to show off his figure. Ruzante instructs him to trot and then to run, to demonstrate his youthfulness. Unable to maintain that level of agility, Tomao falls. After praising his master's form, Ruzante reveals that the final complaint he heard is that Tomao is stingy. His master, stung, swears that Doralice can have all the clothes and money she wants and manage everything that is his. On his way to tell her, Ruzante comments, "Great stories really happen, and whoever tells this won't find a soul who believes him: an old man, who has eighty years hanging from his ass, falls in love" (*RT,* 823).

The following act opens with the instructions of Ginevra, the woman from Ancona, to her maid Ghitta to remember her male disguise and not to slip up by acknowledging in any way that they are women. (The audience learned in the prologue that Ginevra had fallen in love with Gismondo and dressed as a man to follow "him.") Ghitta warns her mistress that the student garb the latter is wearing may bring some unwanted advances from professors and students, who are more interested in young men than in women. Ginevra calls her a beast and tells her to shut up. She proposes that they ask the next passerby their question, but pretend that it is about her brother. At that moment Ruzante leaves Doralice's house.

Observing the two men, and commenting to himself that their bodies don't look complete, Ruzante greets them. Ginevra asks him if he has seen three youths asking to be ransomed and says that one is her brother. When Ruzante asks which one, she describes his courtly refinement. Ruzante counters by mocking his pallid scrawniness and pretends that the youth is still with his mistress. Miserable, Ginevra reveals to Ruzante that she is a young, rich widow from Ancona in love with Gismondo. She promises Ruzante a reward if he can succeed in luring Gismondo away from his mistress, which he craftily assures her he can do.

As soon as they have left, Ruzante exults over his good fortune and laughs at Ginevra's making the same mistake as his mistress. He has heard that love is a little blindfolded boy with wings, but he believes, and is willing to debate with any literary person or even Aristotle, that it is power and desire, and that one draws the other.[12] No one has ever heard of a female animal going after another female animal, and that's the proof. For himself, he's going to go after some of that money.

Ginevra expresses to Ghitta her fear that the other woman will be able to hold Gismondo. Ghitta assures her that Ruzante would not have promised he could bring her the youth if he hadn't had good reason and tells her that her worries are imaginary.

Ruzante relates his encounter with Ginevra to Gismondo, though choosing not to reveal that the stranger is a woman. Ginevra and Ghitta join them, and, as soon as Ginevra has given him money to tailor a pair of pants and a jacket, Ruzante exits in haste to avoid being present when Gismondo's gender is discovered. Ginevra reveals to her beloved that she was born in Gaeta but fled her family, and was married and widowed in quick succession. She declares her love, and her conviction that they have met before. Gismondo admits that she is really Isotta. The two discover that they are twin sisters separated in youth. The shocked Ghitta marvels, "So the object of my mistress's love is her sister? What novel case is this? Whoever said that this took place in Padua would be called a liar. But that's the way it is" (*RT,* 845).

Tomao laments that he has lost his investment and a potential shoulder to cry on with the change of Gismondo to Isotta. Ruzante is too ecstatic over Bessa's declaration of love and their imminent tryst to sympathize with his master's worries. Tomao tries to pry out of him the details of the encounter, but instead is regaled with a lengthy account of Ruzante and Bessa's love story. After Ruzante lost his interest in animals, he began to court girls, going far away to country fairs. On the road he met a wolf once, who tried to scare him, but Ruzante made a loud noise. Imitating it, he makes Tomao jump. He met Bessa there, and they saw each other in church and whispered words of love instead of prayers, and they danced together at festivals. At one of them, he bought her a whole lapful of cookies and doughnuts.[13] But then the wars came; she escaped, and the Germans caught him. She is Doralice's maid, and because she remembered the doughnuts she was willing to speak to her mistress on Tomao's behalf.

Ruzante also tells Tomao that when the latter sees Doralice, to win her favors, he must tell her that when his wife is dead he will marry her and she will live like a lady. He must speak to her when she is on her balcony because city neighbors gossip if a woman lets a man into the house. To quiet Tomao's fears that someone in Doralice's family will wound him, Ruzante devises a plan whereby he will first talk to her. If he sings, Tomao may speak with her, too; if not, he should make himself scarce.

Ginevra and Isotta, meanwhile, plan their future together. Isotta recommends that they marry to spare themselves neighbors' chatter and loneliness in old age. The perfect candidates for grooms are Tancredi and Teodoro, whom she has had a chance to observe during their time together. Since she is in love with Tancredi and both men are from Sicily and very rich, Ginevra should marry Teodoro. They will then go home together and enjoy what is theirs.

Tomao and Doralice manage to speak, despite Ruzante's efforts to interrupt them with hints that someone is coming. Tomao swears to do whatever he can to stop the evil gossip. When he becomes absorbed in erotic baby talk, Doralice heeds Ruzante's warning and disappears. Tomao brags that while she first was interested in him for his money, she is now in love with him. Ruzante's words appear to agree with this assessment, but his sarcastic tone denies it. Ruzante then tells of the plan for the two couples to meet at Arquà if a certain debt of Doralice's can be paid first, quoting a round sum in large coins. Tomao gives it to him to convey to Doralice.

Tancredi proposes to Isotta, Ginevra, and Teodoro that, having lost much time in finding each other, they multiply their enjoyment by sharing their love. He quotes the vernacular proverb, saying that they will be four bodies and one soul. The others agree. In gratitude to the generosity of Padua (Venice in the other version), he offers a prayer that the city always enjoy honor, peace, and abundance, and be protected from its malign neighbors. The four depart.

Ruzante is joined briefly by Menato, and they sing a song in four parts under Bessa's window.[14] In a hurry, and apparently jealous of his friend's success, Menato attempts to depart, but is persuaded by Ruzante to sing one last song. Ruzante then regales him with an account of how much he eats and how both his crazy master and mistress are in love. Menato agrees that his friend eats well, like a draft horse with his head in the sack, and tells Ruzante to stay where he is while he goes on his way. After Menato leaves, Ruzante curses Menato for wanting him to remain. The appearance of Bessa soon soothes him, however.

On his way home, Ruzante meets Tomao and they agree that the master will prepare his things while the servant keeps watch for the women so they may all go on the same boat. Then they will reverse roles as Ruzante goes home to fetch their things. Convinced that Tomao's wife has plans of her own, Ruzante does not share his master's worry that she will not let him go. After Tomao has left, he thinks of the festivals where he will dance and the outfit he will have made from the money the Anconitan woman gave him and what he stole from Tomao: a pair of parti-colored pants, a jacket, and a red hat with a feather. The clothes and his robust figure will attract the girls for a thousand miles around. He will add a sword to make sure he appears worthy of their love.[15]

Tomao has his own sartorial plan: wooden clogs, nightcap, and heavy slippers, complete with salve jars and chamber pot. Ruzante runs home and returns grumbling about the load of junk his master has made him carry and the rush his mistress was in to get him out of the house. As he and Tomao make their way awkwardly toward the boat, Tomao pesters him about whether he has brought everything. Ruzante responds with false assurances, to keep them moving. Finally he interrupts. "We're going the wrong way, the clap on curved swords and straight ones. Let's go this way, it's shorter" (*RT,* 881). Tomao follows him into the wings.

Analysis. The *Woman from Ancona* pushes the premise of the Plautine works to its final conclusion, that the lower-order characters control the workings of society despite the apparent power of their superiors.[16] The problem of the tryst is solved by Bessa, who, of all Beolco's characters, most resembles his putative mother. Through her, he completes the inversion of aristocratic values that has dominated his artistic career. The secret of her power is her ability to acknowledge the truth. Occupying (as woman, peasant, and servant) the lowest social rung, Bessa is able to state simply that she wishes to meet Ruzante in the country and that the best way to accomplish that goal is for Tomao to pay her mistress's debt. Facing no loss of status in recognizing those aspects of reality that the aristocratic system has classified as low, she is not concerned with what the neighbors will think of her, an unmarried woman, nor is she ashamed that Doralice's motive for sleeping with a repulsive old man is money.

In this connection, the presence of Bibbiena's *Calandria* in the play, as in the *Moscheta,* is important.[17] Both plays confront the failure of the male-dominated aristocratic system to maintain its control of society and note that the compensatory obsession with the pleasures of love, which both results from the failure and intensifies it, inverts the social order by debilitating men and locating women and servants at the center of the action. Beolco's solution is the more extreme. While Bibbiena eventually affirms conventional marriage as good, Beolco's characters subvert it. The four aristocratic lovers consent to a highly unconventional pact of (possibly incestuous and homosexual) open marriage very different from their Neoplatonic vocalizations. In fact, the "great" and "beautiful story" to which Beolco so unusually alerted his audience in the prologue and throughout the play is that the upper class is incapable of recognizing a simple difference of gender and the most elemental incest taboos (4.2). Tomao and his wife go their separate ways in extramarital affairs. Free from distortions induced by literary conceits, the peasant servants follow older, more natural patterns, forming an attachment on the basis of attraction that might or might not lead to a more permanent relationship.

Ruzante's famous explanation of his name further supports such an analysis. Padoan, noting its similarity to a passage in Boccaccio's *Comedy of the Fiesolan Nymphs,* discerned in it "the transference of a resumed realism to a literary plane, by means of the superimposition of a cultured explanation."[18] A comparison of the Boccaccian and Beolchian texts, however, shows that the playwright (as has been demonstrated in other cases) did not slavishly copy from his source, but chose a text sympathetic to his polemic and adapted it, emphasizing the primacy of nature over culture.

In the Boccaccio story, Ameto concludes a sweaty day of hunting by playing roughly with his dogs, but abruptly stops when he hears the harmonious voices of a group of maidens. Attracted to their company, he is civilized by their tales of courtly love. The itinerary of Beolco's character is the opposite. His point of departure is the distinguished name of an early Christian bishop, which the character forfeits through sexual activities with animals. His final rejection of the civilizing process comes in his liaison with Bessa, whose name also strongly connects her with the semiwild world of the farm where the constant association of humans and beasts blurs the distinctions between them. The character moves thus not from Ruzante to Perduoçimo, as Padoan maintains, but vice versa.

Fundamental to an understanding of Beolco's attitude is the meaning of the verb *ruzare.* In Veneto dialects, as is clear from Tomao's comment, it refers to a sound, frequently a menacing one (an aspect directly related to the violence in many of Beolco's works). It is only in Tuscan (*ruzzare*) that the verb takes on sexual connotations,[19] implying that Beolco's choice of it was a knowing mockery of those who espoused Tuscan as a vehicle of cultural purity and the medium of Neoplatonic love. Similarly, his location of the tryst in Arquà, home of Petrarch, may be read as a satire of the highly idealized form of love espoused by that poet and his followers, as well as a proprietary claim to refashion the kind of love to be celebrated in the Euganean village that was the site of the land whose rents Beolco was assigned for his severance sum.

The final act of the play concentrates on the only characters of genuine interest to Beolco, the realistic group.[20] Its last scene brings that symmetry with his early works that has been noted elsewhere, in this case with the *Pastoral.* Using his wits to wrest control of the situation from the crotchety authority figure, Ruzante returns to the country whence he came, in search of the freedom and loving intimacy that elude him.

Ruzante's Letter to Sir Marco Alvarotto

Manuscripts, Date, Performances, and Content. Beolco's final work takes the form of a letter to his long-time stage partner, Marco Alvarotto, dated Epiphany (6 January) 1536. Thus the only dating question is that of the calendrical system used by the author. The year would correspond to 1537 if it were dated in the Venetian system, but would remain 1536 in both the Paduan system (which changes the year at Christmas) and the common (New Year) style. One of Beolco's most popular pieces, the *Letter* exists in four manuscript copies and numerous early printings. While no evidence of a performance remains, Zorzi has plausibly proposed that the *Letter* is actually a theatrical monologue that Beolco arranged with Alvarotto to read at the *veglia* or fireside entertainment offered to a hunting party.[21]

Having thanked Alvarotto for his account of the fun that the members of Cornaro's circle are having at the hunt, Beolco describes a recent pleasure of his. He had been thinking of the beauty of this world and wishing he could stay here forever. To do so, he realized, he would have to find a life that made his life even longer than the sober man's life. He asked his books, and they agreed that it was possible for him to achieve his goal, though he would first have to find a lady that some call Lady Sophrosina and others Lady Temperance, whom the ancient magicians had followed. When he asked for proof that some of her ancient devotees were still alive, the books equivocated, saying only that the deaths of three had not yet been reported.[22] He shot back, "Brother books, you're fibbing" (*RT,* 1229). But, knowing that they were good men, he kept looking through them for this woman whom he could court until she gave him a life that would never come unscrewed.[23]

Tired by his fruitless search, he uttered an oath and stretched out on the ground to wait for his dogs to bring back a hare. After sleep had entered his eyes and closed him out of himself,[24] Uncle Paul (the much loved and lamented mainstay of the group) appeared to him. Speaking in country dialect, he declared that even if Ruzante looked in his books as hard as his hounds ran after the hare, he would never find this lady, because the wrong name had been given to him. He then offered to show Ruzante the way to the court that she established for good guys.

"Don't you know that a good natural is better than a hundred nasty old books?" Paul chided him. "Because naturalness existed before them, and they learned from her . . . and she taught me about the woman you're look-

ing for . . . whose real name is Lady Mirth" (*RT,* 1229–31). Lady Mirth
lengthens life by adding to the trunk, rather than attaching one thin life to
the end of another. "But if someone lived just one year and knew he was
alive, wouldn't his life be greater and longer than that of someone who
lived a thousand years and never knew he was alive?"

Lady Mirth harvests this life from her farm, where "the most beautiful
family of men and women that you ever heard of" cultivates it, and the
more she gives away, the more there is to give (*RT,* 1233). Her farm includes flowering hills, and woods, and green fields where lives grow without being planted and the only work is gathering them. The alert lady who
walks along the fence is Aunt Wisdom, who keeps out those who would
damage the lives.[25] Mirth's brother Laughter rolls on the ground, near
Party, a fancily dressed lady with a lap full of cookies and doughnuts, and
her sweaty brother Dance.[26] The four who act as one are Unison Singing,
while the others who are less than nine but more than three are the Pals.
Peace and Charity are taking turns giving one another piggyback rides. A
sharp sound, more beautiful than any Christeleison or Gloria,[27] heralds
Hunt chasing away the enemies of Mirth.

The family members stay outside until dark, then go in to a supper prepared by Appetite, after which they are entertained by Games like Blind
Man's Bluff and Storytelling. Vigil comes with fruit and drinks. Then old
man Rest enters in, painting everyone's eyes, and Silence drives out Noise.
Dream brings fables and tales to make them laugh until Hour is greeted by
Rooster. Awakened, Fun blows on his horn, and the whole family rises to
chase the enemies of Mirth, who have been slinking around the fence like
hungry wolves.

Wrath has been shaking the lives, but Hunt will chase her and Melancholy
away with the hounds Wary and Remedy. But the one who causes the most
damage to the lives is Love, the little boy with the bow and arrows. He's not
the good Love, son of Drive and Fertility, but the son of Damnation and Per-
dition, and is followed by Jealousy. The strange genies that swarm about like
those around Padua the first year after the rout (of Agnadello) are Bothers
and Worries, accompanied by Sorrow and Fantasy, who never rests because
she always wants to be someone else.

Paul cautions his friend not to look at them any more, or he will lose his
ability to see Mirth, whom they must now seek. In simply looking at her,
Ruzante will lengthen his life. He will feel as if buckets of pleasure have been
poured over him, filling his body, protecting him from Love, and making his
life better than a pope's. Each of her words, more musical than pipes and
sweeter than honey, will add a life or a hundred lives and turn everything to

lives, so that he is surrounded by nothing but heaven and lives. While Paul was saying this, Ruzante heard a sweet music and seemed to see Mirth's family form one beautiful thing. He stared at it so hard that his eyes flew open and he realized that it had been the sound and sight of his hounds chasing the hare past him.

Beolco exhorts his friend to share his fun with their pals. He closes the letter with a courteous greeting to "him who is my lord" (Cornaro), which, in its contrast with the rudeness of masters to servants in the late plays, almost seems a pointed lesson in manners. He signs the letter "Your brother, Ruzante."

Analysis.   Almost as if fearing that people would not see beneath his usual theatrical mask, Beolco in this letter (which Grabher termed his literary will)[28] wore one that was completely congruous with his philosophy of the natural. He bypassed the social and cultural establishment with which he had long been in conflict by directing his words to an equal whose friendship dated to his early rebellious days. In a similar way, he eluded the hunting party centering on Cornaro that Alvarotto described to him. Although various reasons for Beolco's absence from the hunt have been advanced, including illness and business, that fact that his letter concerns an episode in Este but was sent from Padua indicates that his movement in that period was not confined. Perhaps his absence was simply the result of an exasperation with Cornaro that paralleled Ruzante's with Tomao, and a need to reestablish his own identity in the face of his master's oppressive normativity. Such an interpretation is supported by the form of the work, which is not a play involving many actors, but a monologue starring Ruzante.

The solitude of the letter indicates that Beolco had searched everything he could of life for the happiness he craved. Aware of his own mortality, he was disappointed both with the unfulfilled promises of the meager sober life of self-denial that Cornaro propounded as a means for attaining old age, and the vague magical (apparently cabalistic) formulas found in books. He turned to his memories of Paul, the man who appears to have inspired him in his early days, and regained his youthful ideal of a country world that, undisturbed by urban interference, maintains its harmony and productivity.

Lady Mirth's farm provided Beolco with a permanent accommodation for the rather schizoid worldview that had characterized much of his work. All the emotions that enhance vitality dwell within its territory; those that would destroy it are fenced out and hunted down. But perhaps the most important aspect of this world is that it is presided over by a personification of motherly peasant goodness and fertility who, like the dog who did not bark in the night, does not appear. I take this to imply that at the center of Beolco's unhappiness was the disappearance of his mother from his infancy, a gap that was never filled, even in the dream, where the final vision is shattered by the pack of hounds who pursue the fleeing hare, like his half brothers pursuing their inheritance (cf. *RT,* 1258–59).

The letter also serves as a vehicle for a final statement on several cultural issues, beginning with the scornful rejection of Cornaro's thin little life that is barely distinguishable from death. Cupid and the artificial nonlove that he represents are dismissed in similar terms. Books are shown to be the pupils, not the teachers, or real life experience.

But perhaps the most important issue is Beolco's move beyond the limits of the Christian religion. There is no figure that corresponds to the Judeo-Christian God, and the allegorical personifications are entirely secular. The location of the farm in a dream, like Nale's made-up tale of the infernal regions, calls into question the immortality of the soul, an ambiguity moving toward unbelief. The letter's closing vision laicizes the Mystical Rose formed by the saints in Dante's vision of heaven by substituting everyday pleasures for divine ones.[29] Beolco's is, in short, a nontheistic paradise in which the common woman and man take the place of God (as the contrast with Dante's Paradise shows), a development that would come to fruition in the nineteenth century.[30] Marisa Milani has aptly observed that Beolco uses Paul "as his spokesman, almost as if he did not have the courage to assume himself the full responsibility for an open profession of 'paganism,' which we must consider the *Letter* to be."[31]

Chapter Eight
The Legacy of Beolco

Late in his life, Beolco belonged to the Academy of the Enflamed (Accademia degli Infiammati), a literary and theatrical group formed around Alvise Cornaro. In the spring of 1542, Cornaro, Beolco and the Sienese Alessandro Piccolomini were readying the first performance of Sperone Speroni's new (and, it would turn out, controversial) tragedy *Canace*. On 17 March Beolco's premature death permanently halted their preparations.[1]

The long silence that had preceded the playwright's death was intimately related to an artistic and intellectual crisis (as Borsellino has noted), as well as to his growing activity in land management. Yet it also reflected the decrease in freedom of expression resulting from the incipient Counter-Reformation and the political alliance of pope and emperor.[2] In such a climate Beolco could neither continue his protests against official culture nor develop a large group of imitators.

Beolco did, however, have some scattered influence. His parasite Loron, for example, appears to have served as the model for Sguazo in Piccolomini's 1536 *Constant Love (Amor Costante:* 2.8). At midcentury two writers, the Venetian Andrea Calmo and the Vicentine Gian Domenico Maganza (Magagnò), acknowledged their emulation of him. Both wrote in local dialect and chose humble subjects as a way of protesting literary and cultural formalism. Because Calmo was a playwright, his works were more closely intertwined with those of his mentor: he wrote a new version of *Flora's Play,* and the printer Alessi claimed that his *Rhodiana* was a work of Beolco's.[3] Maganza was the best-known member of a Paduan group that wrote poetry in the Ruzantine style, including the four-part *Rhymes of Magagnò, Menon, and Begotto in the Paduan Rustic Language,* which he composed with Agostino Rava (Menon) and Bartolomeo Rustichello (Begotto).[4] Beolco also appeared as a proponent of natural speech in works on the *questione della lingua* or discussion of the form of language to be used in Italy, the most famous being Speroni's *Dialogue of the Languages.*

A permanent place in literary history was assured Beolco by the printing of his late works, probably undertaken at the initiative of Alvise Cornaro. *The*

Girl from Piove was published in 1548 by the renowned Giolito de' Ferrari, to be followed by various Venetian editions of *The Veteran, Weasel,* the *Moscheta,* the *Witty Dialogue, Flora's Play, The Girl from Piove, The Cow Comedy, The Woman from Ancona,* the *Letter to Alvarotto,* the *First* and *Second Orations,* and some songs, all of which appeared between 1551 and 1565. Vicenza proved friendly to Beolco in printings as well as in imitators. After publication ceased in Venice, his works were issued in Vicenza until early in the next century, a project possibly initiated by Maganza, as Zorzi has speculated.[5]

Beolco's most famous follower, however, was Galileo Galilei, who became familiar with the playwright's work when he taught at the University of Padua. The Florentine astronomer, who owned the last Venetian edition of Beolco's plays (as well as all four parts of the *Rhymes*), could quote them by heart. When his discovery of a new star drew criticism from the most eminent contemporary professor of philosophy because it put in doubt the ancient concept that the heavens were unchanging, Galileo defended himself in a dialogue between peasants that he had translated into Ruzantine Paduan, in which "he made a peasant reason better than the celebrated professor."[6]

Various authors of eighteenth-century literary surveys mentioned Beolco in passing, his use of dialect prompting them to declare him difficult to decipher. Louis Riccoboni, son of an Italian actor, devoted several pages to Beolco in his *Histoire du théâtre italien,* his familiarity with the commedia dell'arte leading him to characterize Beolco as a founder of the genre.[7] That interpretation was developed by Maurice Sand and his mother, the novelist George Sand, who discovered Beolco's plays and his character Ruzante during a trip to Italy in about 1858. Like many others of his epoch, Sand was fascinated by Italian improvisational theater and devoted a chapter of his book *Masques et buffons* to the Paduan playwright, quoting at length from the printed plays. Sand and his mother also performed *Weasel* in the theater of their villa at Nohant.[8] The coincidence of their rediscovery of that particular play with the era of mass industrialization confirms the opinion that Beolco's works are liminoid, as Victor Turner has observed that liminoid culture became widespread in the nineteenth century.

Scholarly research in Italy lagged until late in the century, when it received impetus from the wave of regional interest that came as a corrective to the earlier nationalist movement and was supported by the Romantics' rediscovery of folk culture and the positivist interest in facts. In 1885, the Paduan bookseller Orlando Orlandini published a few of Beolco's short works in a pocket-sized edition intended for Carnival revelers masking as peasants. Emilio Lovarini began to publish the fruits of what would be a lifelong search of regional archives and libraries in 1888, with an article on folk songs in the works of Ruzante and other contemporary writers. He and Vittorio Rossi discovered the unpublished plays in the Marciana library, making them available in print for the first time. This work attracted the interest of English-language scholars; Winifred Smith and Kathleen M. Lea summarized and discussed some of Beolco's works in their studies of the commedia dell'arte, though concluding that he was only weakly linked with the genre.[9]

French critic Alfred Mortier wrote the first book-length study of Beolco in 1925, issuing most of the plays in their first foreign translation the following year. Mortier's work produced a wave of popular interest on the continent, matched by enthusiasm in Italy as Lovarini and others translated more of the plays into standard Italian, and performances increased.[10] Beolco's fortune gathered momentum in the period after World War Two, when *The Veteran* and *Weasel* were repeatedly produced in Italy, echoing the sufferings borne in Europe and protesting the monolithic power of Fascism.[11] The freer cultural atmosphere of the 1960s and 1970s encouraged productions of the less severe plays, the *Betia, Flora's Play, The Woman from Ancona*. German and Swedish translations of some plays appeared.[12] Beolco found his modern directors in Gianfranco De Bosio, Gigi Giaretta and Giovanni Poli, who, working respectively with the Teatro Stabile di Torino, the Ruzzantini, and the Teatro Universitario di Ca' Foscari, staged the plays with seriousness and creativity, De Bosio taking them as far as the U.S.S.R.[13] Recently the neglected question of incorporating peasant realism into the staging of the plays has received important and innovative attention from Giovanni Calendoli in his ground-breaking productions of the *First Oration* and pre-Ruzantine Paduan peasant literature. Calendoli has also been a central figure in the organization of the international conferences on Beolco conducted under the aegis of the city of Padua.[14]

Scholarly research progressed during this period. Numerous articles and monographs elucidated Beolco's works and their contribution to Western literature, particularly in their evocation of the authentic experience of ordinary human beings, a trend in which the studies of Grabher, Baratto, Borsellino, and Calendoli figured importantly. Vital historical information was added by Menegazzo and Sambin. A high point in Beolco scholarship was reached with Ludovico Zorzi's publication of the first edition of the complete works in 1967. Giorgio Padoan has opened the inquiry into the dating of the works, stimulating other research on the subject.[15]

Beolco's plays were also translated into English during times of social change: the Depression, the period after World War Two, and the late 1960s. It is significant that the most widely available of them was published in the anthology edited by Eric Bentley, who according to Michael Bertin found "the artistry, dynamic and subversive power of the philosophically, politically, and socially radical modernist playwrights irresistible."[16] The first English monograph on Beolco, *Arcadia and the Stage* by Nancy Dersofi (1978), stresses the theatrical and musical aspects of the plays. The research of the present writer explores Beolco's efforts at restructuring society through theater, a forum that allowed him the opportunity to appeal directly to the common humanity of his audience.

Notes and References

English translations from foreign-language sources, unless otherwise noted, are mine.

Chapter One

1. For material in this paragraph see Emilio Lovarini, "Notizie sui parenti e sulla vita del Ruzzante," in *Studi sul Ruzzante e la letteratura pavana,* ed. Gianfranco Folena (Padua: Antenore, 1965), 4–6; Paolo Sambin, "Lazzaro e Giovanni Francesco Beolco, nonno e padre del Ruzante," in *Italia Medioevale e Umanistica* 7 (1964): 136; cf. David Herlihy, "Popolazione e strutture sociali dal XV al XVI secolo," in *Tiziano e Venezia* (Vicenza: Neri Pozza, 1980), 71–74.

2. Material in this and following paragraph from Sambin, "Lazzaro," 134–36, 152–54; Lovarini, "Notizie," 6–7; for citizenship see James Grubb, "Alla ricerca delle prerogative locali: la cittadinanza a Vicenza, 1404–1509," *Civis* 8 (1984): 177–91.

3. Material in this paragraph from Sambin, "Lazzaro," 140, 144, 147–51.

4. Sambin, "Lazzaro," 154–56 (which the account of the flight closely follows), 147.

5. For material in this paragraph, see Lovarini, "Notizie," 7–11,16–18, 20; Sambin, "Lazzaro," 151, 153, 157–58, 165–66, and document 6.

6. Historical information closely follows Sambin, "Lazzaro," 163–65, and id., "Briciole biografiche del Ruzante e del suo compagno d'arte Marco Aurelio Alvarotti (Menato)," *Italia Medioevale e Umanistica* 9 (1966): 266–67, adding some interpretive remarks; Sambin's discovery revises the traditional birth date of 1502, based on the tombstone inscription stating that Beolco died in 1542 when he was forty; David Herlihy has shown that rounding off to the nearest decade was common in reports of age: *Medieval Households* (Cambridge: Harvard University Press, 1985), 149.

7. Emilio Menegazzo, "Altre osservazioni intorno alla vita e all'ambiente del Ruzante e di Alvise Cornaro," *Italia Medioevale e Umanistica* 9 (1966): 229; Sambin, "Lazzaro," 167; Lovarini, "Notizie," 18.

8. As characterized by Jackson Cope, "Lives of the Daemon Players: Ruzante to Grimaldi," in *Dramaturgy of the Daemonic* (Baltimore: The Johns Hopkins University Press, 1984), 149, n. 24.

9. See respectively, Robert Finlay, "Al servizio del Sultano: Venezia, i Turchi, e il mondo Cristiano, 1523–1538," in *"Renovatio urbis": Venezia nell'età di Andrea Gritti,* ed. Manfredo Tafuri (Rome: Officina, 1984), 79, and Carlo Dionisotti, "Nota biografica," in Pietro Bembo, *Prose e Rime,* ed. C. Dionisotti, 2nd ed. (Turin: UTET, 1966), 58.

10. Cf. Geza Vermes, "Ancient Judaism in the Light of the Dead Sea Scrolls" and "Rabbinic History" in *Post-Biblical Jewish Studies* (Leiden: Brill, 1975), 3–7, 169–224, for a similar dynamic.

11. Ugo Tucci, "The Psychology of the Venetian Merchant," in *Renaissance Venice*, ed. J. R. Hale (London: Faber and Faber, 1973) 356; Angelo Ventura, *Nobiltà e popolo nella società veneta del '400 e '500* (Bari: Laterza, 1964), 299 for legitimacy, passim for noble control and withdrawal from commerce; Linda Carroll, "Carnival Rites as Vehicles of Protest in Renaissance Venice," *Sixteenth Century Journal* 16 (1985): 487–502; Frederic Lane, "Recent Studies on the Economic History of Venice," *Journal of Economic History* 23 (1963): 324–26; id., "Venetian Shipping during the Commercial Revolution," in *Crisis and Change in the Venetian Economy in the Sixteenth and Seventeenth Centuries*, ed. Brian Pullan (London: Methuen, 1968), 27–28, 33ff. The Venetian economy improved toward the end of the century.

12. For the material here and below, see Finlay, "Al servizio," 79; Lovarini, "Notizie," 26; Thomas Kuehn, "Some Ambiguities of Female Inheritance Ideology in the Renaissance," *Continuity and Change* 2 (1987): 24–25; Sambin, "Briciole," 268–69; for raising, cf. Herlihy, *Medieval,* 153; illegitimates were also prevented from enjoying the benefits of belonging to the artisan class because they had not grown up within that network of associations.

13. For here and below, Lovarini, "Notizie," 7–11, 18; Sambin, "Lazzaro," 150–53 and document 7; Lovarini refers to Giovanni Jacopo writing his will in Melchiorre's house (12), but since the testator was living in the country at the time, this may be Melchiorre's quarters in the Beolco house in Padua.

14. Cf. Ventura, *Nobiltà,* 89; for below, Lovarini, "Notizie," 8–9.

15. Cf. Lovarini, "Notizie," 7–9, 12, 26.

16. Sambin, "Lazzaro," 166–67; the case of Giovanni Francesco also indicates a disturbance; the eldest son, he would ordinarily have borne the name of his grandfather Pietro. Lazzaro's choice of his brother's name for both of his legitimate sons may indicate a break with his father; Giovanni Francesco in turn may have attempted to reestablish the tradition as a way of rebelling against Lazzaro. For name Melchiorre, Luigi Monga, *In the Very Heart of Man: The Life and Poetry of Carlo Porta* (Tampa: University Presses of Florida, 1986), 7; for Beolco descendants, Lovarini, "Notizie," 56; for church post, Emilio Lovarini, "Nuovi documenti sul Ruzzante," in *Studi,* 66–68.

17. Two hundred years later, Venetian political theorist Marco Foscarini would still be preoccupied with justifying the republic's defeat; see his *Necessità della storia e della facoltà di ben dire per gli uomini di Repubblica,* ed. Luisa Ricaldone (Milan: Angeli, 1983), 130ff, 144, 177, 189, and 198; see also Frederic Lane, *Venice* (Baltimore: The Johns Hopkins University Press, 1973), 245.

18. Antonio Bonardi, "I padovani ribelli alla repubblica di Venezia (a. 1509–1530), studio storico con appendice di documenti inediti," *Miscellanea di storia veneta a cura della Deputazione veneta di storia patria,* ser. 2, 8 (1902): 339; for the paragraph below, 387–91, 407, 548, 573.

19. Emilio Menegazzo, "Ricerche intorno alla vita e all'ambiente del Ruzante e di Alvise Cornaro," *Italia Medioevale e Umanistica* 7 (1964): 207–211.

20. Marino Sanuto, *I diarii,* ed. Renato Fulin et al., 58 vols. (Venice: Visentini, 1879–1902), vol. 8, cols. 358, 353, 359; for above, Emilio Lovarini, "Introduzione," in *Antichi testi di letteratura pavana,* ed. E. Lovarini (Bologna: Romagnoli dall'Acqua, 1894), xl.

21. For stretching of leaves, see Bonardi, "Padovani ribelli," 440; for wills, see Sambin, "Lazzaro," 161–62; the conclusions here differ from Sambin's for reasons given in the text.

22. For aunt's will, Lovarini, "Notizie," 7; a further indication that the change excluded Angelo may be found in the fact that he later attempted to claim an annual income from his father's estate, something he might not have done if he were receiving the income from Giovanni Jacopo's legacy; moreover, in the latter instance, although the legitimate heirs agreed to give Angelo a small compromise sum, Giovanni Jacopo later acted for them in contesting Angelo's collection of it. See Menegazzo, "Ricerche," 214, and Sambin, "Altre testimonianze (1525–1540) di Angelo Beolco," *Italia Medioevale e Umanistica* 7 (1964): 236–37 and document 5; the third will may have been influenced by Giovanni Francesco's wife: for the large sums her family borrowed from the Beolcos in 1505, 1506, and 1513 see Lovarini, "Notizie," 22, and for Giovanni Jacopo's final will, 12.

23. Material in this paragraph from Lovarini, "Notizie," 8, 11, 18, 31–32; Sambin, "Lazzaro," 152, 157, and document 7.

Chapter Two

1. Giorgio Padoan, "Angelo Beolco da Ruzante a Perduoçimo," in *Momenti del Rinascimento veneto* (Padua: Antenore, 1978), 96–98, for here and below; Mario Baratto, "L'esordio di Ruzante," in *Tre studi sul teatro* (Venice: Neri Pozza, 1968), 12, for here and below; for the manuscript, Ludovico Zorzi, "Nota al testo," in Angelo Beolco, *Ruzante Teatro,* ed. and trans. L. Zorzi, 2d ed. (Turin: Einaudi, 1967), 1611–12.

2. A problem with this identification is posed by the names of the main characters (Ruzante and Zilio), conflicting with Sanudo's report of Ruzante and Menato (see below). One solution frequently proposed is that the characters were already so well known that their names were used regardless of the specific role.

3. Emilio Lovarini, "Ruzzante a Venezia," in *Studi,* 81–107, from which much of the present information is taken; based on Sanuto, *Diarii,* vol. 28, cols. 254–55, 264.

4. For here and below see Edward Muir, *Civic Ritual in Renaissance Venice* (Princeton: Princeton University Press, 1981), 167–75; see also Stanley Chojnacki, "Political Adulthood in Fifteenth-Century Venice," *American Historical Review* 91 (1986): 791–810.

5. Victor Turner, "Liminal to Liminoid in Play, Flow and Ritual: An Essay in Comparative Symbology," *Rice University Studies* 60 (1974): 53–92; see also Linda

Carroll, "Carnival Rites"; id., "Authorial Defense in Boccaccio and Ruzante: From Liminal to Liminoid," *Romance Quarterly* 34 (1987): 103–16; for Carnival origin of theater: Paolo Toschi, *Le origini del teatro italiano* (1955; Turin: Boringhieri, 1976).

6. Franco Fido has noted that Beolco's career begins and ends with a dream: "An Introduction to the Theater of Angelo Beolco," *Renaissance Drama* 6 (1973): 203–18; the second dream is the *Letter to Alvarotto* discussed below. The inconsistency in verb tenses and colloquial tone of the following plot summary reflects the original.

7. *Ruzante Teatro,* 17; all further quotations will be taken from this source, (hereafter *RT*), with page numbers given in the text.

8. Giorgio Padoan's attempts to reinterpret this passage as referring not to comic writers but to the officials who reopened the university ("Esercizi di restauro della *Pastoral,*" in *Momenti,* 222) distorts the evident meaning of the passage (cf. Baratto, "L'esordio," 13), in particular because the Venetian officials would probably have been associated with the pursuit of fame, a humanistic endeavor particularly cultivated in Venice after the wars, for which see Felix Gilbert, "Biondo, Sabellico and the Beginnings of Venetian Official Historiography," in *Florilegium Historiale: Essays Presented to Wallace K. Ferguson,* ed. J. G. Rowe and W. H. Stockdale (Toronto: University of Toronto Press, 1971), esp. 286.

9. See George Ulysse, "La *Pastoral* del Ruzante e le egloghe pastorali e rusticali dei pre-Rozzi senesi," in *Convegno internazionale di studi sul Ruzante,* ed. Giovanni Calendoli and Giuseppe Vellucci (Venice: Corbo e Fiore, 1987), 75; for literary references, see Baratto, "L'esordio," 11–68; Zorzi, "Note," 1283–309; and Charles E. Fantazzi, "Ruzzante's Rustic Challenge to Arcadia," *Studies in Philology* 82 (1985): 81–103, although some material on Beolco in the latter should be taken with caution; for Arcadian burial rites, see David Quint, "Sannazaro: From Orpheus to Proteus," in *Origin and Originality in the Renaissance* (New Haven: Yale University Press, 1983), 43–80.

10. For this paragraph, see Baratto, "L'esordio," 27–29; Lovarini, *Antichi testi;* Carlo Grabher, *Ruzzante* (Milan-Messina: Principato, 1953), 55.

11. See Linda Carroll, "Carnival Rites"; id., "Who's on Top?: Gender as Societal Power Configuration in Italian Renaissance Painting and Drama," *Sixteenth Century Journal* 20 (1989): 565–92.

12. Padoan, "Angelo," 102–3; Ulysse, "La *Pastoral,*" 73; for the first point only, Ludovico Zorzi, "Nota," in Ruzante, *Vaccaria,* ed. L. Zorzi (Padua: Randi, 1954), 298–99. The remainder of this paragraph summarizes Baratto's interpretation of the play.

13. Baratto, "L'esordio," 62; for following, 55, 62, 65. Baratto's work informs the rest of the section.

14. Suicide is considered a grievous sin by the Catholic Church, which prohibits the bodies of suicides from being buried in consecrated ground; the conflict between Christian values and Arcadia's paganism derives from the participation of

many humanists in the Renaissance religious revival. Cf. Thomas Mayer, "Marco Mantova and the Paduan Religious Crisis of the Early Sixteenth Century," in *Cristianesimo nella storia* 7 (1986): 41–61. For reputation, below, see Gilbert, "Biondo."

15. For a similar episode involving Venetian soldiers, see Felix Gilbert, *The Pope, His Banker, and Venice* (Cambridge: Harvard University Press, 1980), 31–32.

16. He also is the product of theatrical conventions: Baratto, "L'esordio," 27–28, n. 33; Grabher, *Ruzzante*, 55; Zorzi, "Note," 1298–99, n. 112; many scholars have linked his Bergamasque dialect with the Beolco family origin in Milan; Giovanni Francesco had the opportunity to speak Lombard with the Cremonese porter who witnessed a document for him in 1515 (cf. Sambin, "Lazzaro," 179), possibly providing a model for the interaction of Doctor Francesco and Bertuolo.

17. Cf. Sambin, "Lazzaro," 166–67; the widowed sister, who seems added to the text as an embellishment, has no correspondent in Beolco's life, as his half sisters did not marry until later. Lovarini, "Notizie," 24, for names, Lovarini, "Notizie," 43–44; id., "La *Pastorale*," in *Studi*, 287.

18. Baratto, "L'esordio," 43. For the above paragraph, note that Paola Beolco was also probably a speaker of rural dialect.

19. Zorzi, "Note," 1552-53, and "Nota al testo," 1624–26; information in this and the next paragraph is derived from the same source; Dovehouse Books, Toronto, has announced an English translation by Ronald Ferguson and Antonio Franceschetti in the Carleton Renaissance Plays in Translation series.

20. Giovanni Calendoli, *Ruzante* (Venice: Corbo e Fiore, 1985), 71.

21. Sanuto, *Diarii,* vol. 29, cols. 536–37.

22. This and information on Cornaro taken from Sambin, "Briciole," 266, 268–69.

23. The meaning of natural for Beolco is the male organ (cf. p. 414 and the prologue of the *Moscheta*). In the language at large it means illegitimate, and was used in Giovanni Francesco's will with reference to Angelo: Lovarini, "Notizie," 26.

24. It was common humanistic practice to construct false but glorious Roman genealogies for aristocratic families: Zorzi, "Note," 1561. The pox (below) was probably syphilis, a devastating epidemic that appeared in the late fifteenth century: cf. Brian Pullan, *Rich and Poor in Renaissance Venice* (Oxford: Blackwell, 1971), 223 and passim.

25. The first hint of a paganism that will assume a very important place in Beolco's thought.

26. Turner, "Liminal," 75, 72, and esp. 84–89.

27. Calendoli, *Ruzante,* 69.

28. Jose Oliveira Barata, "Sulla cultura del Ruzante," *Atti dell'Istituto Veneto di Scienze, Lettere ed Arti* (Classe di scienze morali, lettere ed arti) 131 (1972–73): 101–14.

29. Ibid., 114.

30. Nino Borsellino, "Ruzzante," in *Enciclopedia dello spettacolo,* 10 vols. (Rome: Le Maschere, 1954–68), 8:1344.

31. Ronald Ferguson, "Moralità convenzionale e moralità naturale in tre commedie del Ruzante," in *Convegno internazionale,* 21–35; the following summarizes his views.

32. Such a solution also handily eliminates the problems of illegitimacy; for data supporting this section, see Linda Carroll, "Ruzante's Early Adaptations from More and Erasmus," *Italica,* 66 (1989): 29–34.

33. Cf. his *Cow Comedy (Vaccaria),* 1141: "a learned man, digging and flipping through many books, finds many things and puts them aside for when he needs them, and they get him something."

Chapter Three

1. Zorzi, "Nota al testo," 1631 (cf. 1616–17).

2. Episodes discussed here because details are used in chronologies. For performances see Sanuto, *Diarii,* vol. 33, col. 9 and vol. 34, col. 124; Lovarini, "Ruzzante a Venezia"; for Contarini, Sanuto, *Diarii,* vol. 12, cols. 277–78. Gasparo di Francesco Alvise Contarini is sometimes mistakenly conflated by scholars with the religious reformer (Gaspare di Alvise). The play was not held in the Crosechieri monastery as is often assumed; it burned in 1514 and was not rebuilt until 1543 (see Silvia Lunardon, "L'ospedale dei Crociferi," in *Hospitale S. Mariae Cruciferorum,* ed. S. Lunardon [Venice: Istituzioni di Ricovero e di Educazione, 1984], 42; for the *Mandragola* see Sanuto, *Diarii,* vol. 32, cols. 458, 466).

3. Giovanni Calendoli has proposed that the aspect of the play causing the scandal was Beolco's efforts to convince the Venetian rulers of the importance and independence of Padua: "Le immagini di Venezia nel primo teatro di Angelo Beolco," in *Convegno internazionale,* 263–73.

4. Robert Finlay, *Politics in Renaissance Venice* (New Brunswick, N.J.: Rutgers University Press, 1980), 156–61.

5. Lovarini, "Notizie," 18–20; Sambin, "Altre testimonianze," 222–23. For army wages see M. E. Mallett and J. R. Hale, *The Military Organization of a Renaissance State* (Cambridge: Cambridge University Press, 1984), 495.

6. Lovarini, *Antichi testi,* xlix–li; id., "L'alfabeto dei villani in pavano," *Studi,* 428–30; M. Cristofari, *Il Codice Marciano It. XI,* 66 (Padua: CEDAM, 1937), 26. After examining the manuscript, I believe the date to read 1524.

7. "Ruzante e la *Lettera amorosa* (migrazione e degradazione dell'emblema di una Compagnia della Calza)," in *Giorgione e la cultura veneta tra '400 e '500,* [ed. Maurizio Calvesi] (Rome: De Luca, 1981), 219–23; Padoan, "Angelo," 108–12.

8. Paola Zambelli, "Many Ends for the World: Luca Gaurico Instigator of the Debate in Italy and in Germany," in *"Astrologi hallucinati": Stars and the End of the World in Luther's Time,* ed. Paola Zambelli (Berlin: de Gruyter, 1986), 246–54.

9. Helga Robinson Hammerstein, "The Battle of the Booklets: Prognostic

Tradition and Proclamation of the Word in Early Sixteenth-Century Germany," in ibid., 137; for rains and Donà see Sanuto, *Diarii*, vol 32., cols. 412, 420, 445.
　10. Cf. Andrea Da Mosto, *I dogi di Venezia* (Milan: Martello, 1966), 282–84.
　11. Zorzi, "Note," 1590–93, n. 1, and 1594, n. 11, for here and below; Giorgio Padoan, "Introduzione," in Angelo Beolco Il Ruzante, *La Pastoral, La Prima Oratione, Una Lettera giocosa* (Padua: Antenore, 1978), 27.
　12. Sanuto, *Diarii*, vol. 37, cols. 559–60, 572. The author of the triple comedy was not Manenti as Padoan contends; part of it at least was the work of Lorenzo Strozzi. Cf. Sergio Bertelli, "Nota al testo," in Niccolò Machiavelli, *Opere*, ed. S. Bertelli, 10 vols. (Milan: Salerno [Verona: Valdonega], 1968–82), 4.172, and "Introduzione," 10.xxi–xxii. Lovarini's interpretation of *autor* as "promoter" (the word's primary meaning) seems more accurate. Cf. Nicola Zingarelli, *Vocabolario della lingua italiana*, 10th ed. (Bologna: Zanichelli, 1970), 150. The rehearsal passage would thus mean that Manenti was the promoter and the "comedy" the evening's entertainment.
　13. For Manenti see Sanuto, *Diarii*, vol. 35, cols. 364–65; for the performance see vol. 37, cols. 559–60. For the letter see Machiavelli, *Opere*, 4.434–35, and Bertelli, "Nota al Testo," 172, "Introduzione," 10.xxi–xxii. For the *Mandragola* in Venice and Manenti's arrival see Sanuto, *Diarii*, vol. 32, cols. 458, 466, 501–504; for Contarini see vol. 36, cols. 265–66. For Manenti as fool (below) see Bernardo Dovizi da Bibbiena, *La Calandria*, 1.3, in *La commedia del Cinquecento*, ed. Guido Davico Bonino, 2 vols. (Turin: Einaudi, 1977), 1.21. The present analysis leaves the meaning of "quel da l'olio" to ongoing research.
　14. E.g., a member of the Bolani family is identified as both Lorenzo and Sebastian, while a painter is called both Marco and Donado (Sanuto, *Diarii*, vol. 16, cols. 675–76 and vol. 17, cols. 17, 40–41, 69, 77); Lorenzo Loredan is identified alternately as grandson and son of the late Doge (vol. 34, cols. 149, 164), etc. For "quel da l'olio" as Manenti see Padoan, "Angelo," 116.
　15. Based on Sambin, "Altre testimonianze," 221–23, "Briciole," 278, 267; Menegazzo, "Ricerche," 211–14; Lovarini, "Notizie," 30–32; Herlihy, "Popolazione."
　16. Sanuto, *Diarii*, vol. 40, cols. 789–90, summarized in the following paragraph; Lovarini, "Ruzzante a Venezia," 94–96, 100–3, whose conclusions are accepted here.
　17. Sanuto, *Diarii*, vol. 41, col. 366 (cf. vol. 34, col. 348). For the alliance see Garrett Mattingly, *Renaissance Diplomacy* (Harmondsworth: Penguin, 1955), 165. The present study forms part of a larger project that traces the political positions of Venetian aristocrats who invited Beolco to Venice or followed his performances, and compares them with the opinions expressed in the plays.
　18. Giandomenico Maganza, "Al clarissimo Cavalier Mozzenigo,"in *Il fiore della lirica veneziana*, ed. Manlio Dazzi, 2 vols. (Venice: Neri Pozza, 1956), 1.296. Padoan's contention that Beolco did return to Venice ("Angelo," 146, n. 170; "Fiorina nel mondo degli uomini," in *Convegno internazionale*, 55) is based on an erroneous reading of the line in the Maganza poem that says that Beolco would not

have passed Lizzafusina, the port on the mainland whence ferries carried people to and from Venice. Padoan supposes that Beolco would have been going toward Venice, but earlier Maganza states, "I know that Padua would never have heard him." Cf. Sanuto, *Diarii,* vol. 18, col. 358, for "pasar Lisa Fusina," meaning "head toward the mainland." For permission, Muir, *Civic Ritual,* 168–69.

19. The above is based on Sambin, "Altre testimonianze," 223–27 and document 2; id., "Briciole," 272–73, 277–78; Menegazzo, "Ricerche," 210–11; Emmanuele Cicogna, *Delle iscrizioni veneziane,* 6 vols. (Venice: Orlandelli, 1842), 6.2.690, n. 1; and Lovarini, "Notizie," 31, with the addition of some interpretive remarks.

20. This paragraph summarizes Emilio Lovarini, "La *Betia,*" in *Studi,* 293–317; id., "Per l'edizione critica del testo," in *Studi,* 136–44; id., "Ruzzante a Venezia," 88–94; Padoan, "Angelo," 112–122; Zorzi, "Note," 1310–14 and "Nota al testo," 1612–15. The *Betia* is the only one of Beolco's plays to have been filmed: Gianfranco De Bosio, "Un trentennio di lavoro sul Ruzante," in *Convegno internazionale,* 233.

21. Calendoli has given a more accurate interpretation of them as adjustments to the script by the actor-author during rehearsals (*Ruzante,* 47; cf. Zorzi, "Nota al testo," 1613).

22. Bonardi, "Padovani ribelli," 384; cf. Gilbert, *Pope,* 22.

23. For Betta, *bettagna,* see G. B. Pellegrini, "Il dialetto bellunese-friulano," in *Studi di dialettologia e filologia veneta* (Pisa: Pacini, 1977), 255; cf. "*bestiata* = "terrible beast" in S. Domini, A. Fulizio, A. Miniussi, and G. Vittori, *Vocabolario fraseologico del dialetto "bisiac"* (Bologna: Cappelli, 1985); "*betola*" = "tavern" in R. Naccari and G. Boscolo, *Vocabolario del dialetto chioggiotto* (Chioggia: Charis, 1982).

24. Salvatore Di Maria, "Blame-by-praise Irony in the *Ecatommiti* of Giraldi Cinzio," *Quaderni d'Italianistica* 6.2 (1985): 178–92.

25. Bonardi, "Padovani ribelli," 433, 447–48.

26. The translation is Fido's: "Introduction," 207.

27. A satire of the Neoplatonic belief that love produces four souls by the dwelling of each in that of the lover, a belief that will be given definitive form by Leone Ebreo in the *Dialoghi d'amore,* first published in 1535 but at least partially extant in manuscript form since early in the century; see chapter 7, *The Woman from Ancona.*

28. Grabher, *Ruzzante,* 66ff, and Baratto, "L'esordio," 60–61.

29. Linda Carroll, "Authorial Defense"; id., "Carnival Rites."

30. For the *mariazo* see most recently Marisa Milani, "La tradizione del 'mariazo' nella letteratura pavana," in *Convegno internazionale,* 105–15.

31. Cf. Finlay, "Al servizio," 80.

32. Sanuto, *Diarii,* vol. 8, col. 308; vol. 14, cols. 262, 333, 593; vol. 18, col. 366; vol. 19, cols. 67, 69, 239, 267, 286; vol. 21, col. 229; vol. 24, cols. 266, 593; vol. 27, cols. 623, 624, 660; vol. 28, cols. 55, 125, 217, 256, 320, 394, 543, 548,

562; vol. 30, cols. 433, 439; vol. 32, cols. 130, 319; vol. 33, cols. 254, 274, 275, 277, 311, 313, 335, 495, 544, 636; for scandalous office-buying see Finlay, *Politics,* 196–226.

33. The commemoration of its date, for example, became a Venetian state feast during his dogeship, fifteen years after the fact. For art and Carnival, Edward Muir, "Images of Power: Art and Pageantry in Renaissance Venice," *American Historical Review* 84 (1979): 16–52; for France and centralized government, Carroll, "Who's on Top?"; for League of Cognac, Finlay, "Al servizio," 82–83.

34. Grabher, *Ruzzante,* 84–85, 91.

35. Quote from Monga, *In the Very Heart,* 120, n. 18, and see 43–44; Mikhail Bakhtin, *Rabelais and His World,* trans. Helene Iswolsky (Cambridge: MIT Press, 1968).

36. For references to Bembo see Zorzi's notes; for the importance of love cf. Gaetano Cozzi, "La donna, l'amore e Tiziano," *Tiziano e Venezia,* 47–63; data on Bembo's life from Dionisotti, "Nota biografica," 57–60; see also Carroll, "Authorial Defense"; for satire of Bembo see Fido, "Introduction," 206.

37. Bembo, *Asolani* in *Prose e Rime,* 499.

38. Cf. prologue, 149, 153, and "The Praise of Folly," in *The Essential Erasmus,* trans. and ed. John P. Dolan (New York: New American Library of World Literature, 1964), 124; Zorzi ("Note," 1314) notes a resemblance to Sannazaro; however, while Sannazaro stresses the human observer, Beolco and Erasmus focus on the creatures. The present analysis first appeared in Carroll, "Ruzante's Early Adaptations."

39. For which see Eugenio Battisti, *L'antirinascimento* (Milan: Feltrinelli, 1962), 469.

40. Fido, "Introduction," 215; for fennel, Carlo Ginzburg, *The Night Battles,* trans. John and Anne Tedeschi (Baltimore: Johns Hopkins University Press, 1983), 4 and passim.

41. Sperone Speroni, *Opere* (Venice, 1740), 1.114; quoted in Lovarini, "Notizie," 38; Maganza, "Al clarissimo Cavalier," 296.

42. Lovarini, "Notizie," 33ff; Menegazzo, "Ricerche," 212–13; Gianfranco Folena, "Nota," in Lovarini, *Studi,* 60; for Speroni on gold see *Opere,* 5.320 (cited in Ventura *Nobiltà,* 331–32).

43. For the leisured gentleman see Angelo Ventura, *Nobiltà,* 36–37, 51–52, 55ff, 78, 187–88, 198–99, 236–37, 331–32, 375–76; and Gilbert, *Pope,* passim. For wages see Mallett and Hale, *Military Organization,* 494–95. For split in upper classes see Gaetano Cozzi, "La giustizia e la politica agli albori dell' età moderna," in *Repubblica di Venezia e Stati Italiani* (Turin: Einaudi, 1982), 88ff.

Chapter Four

1. Emilio Lovarini, "I prologhi della *Moschetta,*" *Studi,* 327–30; Zorzi, "Nota al testo," 1619; Padoan, "Angelo," 149–58.

2. For famine see Pullan, *Rich and Poor,* 240–50; for Ariosto, Angela

Casella, "Presentazione," in L. Ariosto, *Commedie,* ed. A. Casella, G. Ronchi, E. Varasi, *Tutte le Opere* 4 (Milan: Mondadori, 1974), xxviii.

3. Cristoforo da Messisbugo, *Libro Novo/nel quale s'insegna/A far d'ogni sorte di vivanda* . . . (Venice, 1564), fols. 9r, 18r; reprinted as *Banchetti, composizioni di vivande e apparecchio generale,* ed. Fernando Bandini (Venice: Neri Pozza, 1960). For land documents see Archivio di Stato di Padova, Archivio Notarile, vol. 2735, fols. 113v, 124, 125, 134.

4. For illustrations see Linda Carroll, "Linguistic Variation and Social Protest in the Plays of Ruzante," *Allegorica* 8 (1983): 211.

5. As Lovarini noted, the prologues of the *Moscheta* are unusual because they contain specific references to the play. Beolco's earlier prologues—those of the *Betia,* for example—were general statements of his polemic and could be recited independently.

6. Zorzi ("Note," 1453, n. 10, and 1468, n. 19) defines them as headgear, but, in the context, a gather of cloth resembling a bustle but running entirely around the skirt, a popular fashion of the time, seems more likely (cf. in Zorzi the illustrations opposite pp. 76 and 1196).

7. See Carroll, "Ruzante's Early Adaptations"; cf. Frank E. Manuel and Fritzie P. Manuel, "Sketch for a Natural History of Paradise," in *Myth, Symbol, and Culture,* ed. Clifford Geertz (New York: Norton, 1971), 114 and Norman Cohn, *The Pursuit of the Millennium,* 2d ed. (New York: Oxford University Press, 1970), passim.

8. See Diane Owen Hughes, "Earrings for Circumcision: Distinction and Purification in the Italian Renaissance City," in *Persons in Groups: Social Behavior as Identity Formation in Medieval and Renaissance Europe,* ed. Richard C. Trexler (Binghamton, N.Y.: Center for Medieval and Early Renaissance Studies, State University of New York, 1985), esp. 165–70: the Este played a key role in the process; Stanley Chojnacki, "La posizione della donna a Venezia nel Cinquecento," *Tiziano e Venezia,* esp. 69–70.

9. Cf. Natalie Zemon Davis, "Women on Top," *Society and Culture in Early Modern France* (Stanford: Stanford University Press, 1975), 124–51; Carroll, "Who's on Top?"

10. Cf. Giuseppe Calò, *Ciò: Zibaldone veneziano* (Venice: Corbo e Fiore, 1986), 143, "musina" or piggybank for the female genitals.

11. Cf. Walter Gibson, "Bruegel, Dulle Griet, and Sexist Politics in the Sixteenth Century," in *Pieter Bruegel und seine Welt,* ed. Otto von Simson and Matthias Winner (Berlin: Gebr. Mann, 1979), 9–15.

12. Oliver Logan, *Culture and Society in Venice 1470–1790* (London: Batsford, 1972), 32, and see 31; material on *Oration,* Zorzi, "Note," 1568, 1570, notes 1 and 5; id., "Nota al testo," 1626–27 for manuscript.

13. Pullan, *Rich and Poor,* 241–44.

14. Sambin, "Altre testimonianze," 233, 231–32; Cornaro was related to but not part of the Venetian patrician family (Menegazzo, "Ricerche," 210–11).

15. Menato, apparently a silent accompanist (Zorzi, "Note," 1570, n. 7).

16. For usury see Archivio di Stato di Venezia, Consiglio dei Dieci, Capi, Lettere dei Rettori (Padova), busta 81, fol. 54; for grain disturbances see fols. 48, 49, 54, 75, 79; Sanuto, *Diarii,* vol. 48, col. 59; Mario Prosperi, *Angelo Beolco nominato Ruzante* (Padua: Liviana, 1970), notes that in 1455 Jews had been expelled from Padua and moved to rural towns (85); if they converted to escape the heavy taxes imposed upon Jews, they were required to give up their goods to avoid competing with Christian merchants (90).

17. Grabher, *Ruzzante,* 244; for analysis below see Linda Carroll, "Correlates of Emotion in Ruzante," in *The Eleventh LACUS Forum 1984,* ed. Robert A. Hall, Jr. (Columbia, S.C.: Hornbeam Press, 1985), 380–82; for Cornaro, cf. Zorzi, "Note," 1568, n. 1.

18. Cf. John Martin, "The Sect of Benedetto Corazzaro," Div. on Reformation, Ritual, and the Millennium in Venice, Sixteenth Century Studies Conference, 30 October 1987; see also Angelo Beolco, *The Girl from Piove,* 947.

19. J. H. Hexter, *The Vision of Politics on the Eve of the Reformation* (New York: Basic Books, 1973), 14.

20. Gaetano Cozzi, "La politica del diritto nella Repubblica di Venezia," in *Repubblica,* 327.

21. William Bouwsma, *Venice and the Defense of Republican Liberty* (Berkeley and Los Angeles: University of California Press, 1968), 82; for charitable bodies see Pullan, *Rich and Poor,* 258–59; for religious fervor see Prosperi, *Angelo Beolco,* 74–86 (the most extensive discussion of the *Oration*); for criticisms of clerics, see, for example, Gregorio Piaia, *Marsilio da Padova nella Riforma e nella Controriforma* (Padua: Antenore, 1977), 30–31.

22. For indulgences see Zorzi, "Note," 1576–77, n. 30; for soldiers and the Fugger bank see Gilbert, *Pope,* 55, 77.

23. For Padoan's theory see "Angelo," 129–34. Messisbugo's description, quoted by Padoan, excludes his proposal that Beolco recited a monologue at the 24 January 1529 performance, as Messisbugo states that Ruzante and seven fellow performers sang and argued about peasant matters; the number of performers cited by Messisbugo being greater than the number of characters required by the *Witty Dialogue,* the supernumeraries may have served as silent extras, as Menato had in the *Second Oration.*

24. Calendoli, *Ruzante,* 81–93; although Pisani was still a prisoner of the Spanish (Giorgio Padoan, "La guerra della Lega di Cognac nel *Parlamento,*" in *Momenti,* 265), his friends or relatives could have been among the guests; for the 1530 hunt, Sanuto, *Dairii,* vol. 52, cols. 495–96; for Cornaro and Paduan rebels see Menegazzo, "Ricerche," 207–11.

25. Emilio Lovarini, "Profilo del Ruzzante," in *Studi,* 373; Zorzi, "Note," 1620, n. 6; for Cornaro's fame see *Scritti sulla "Vita sobria": Elogio e lettere,* ed. Marisa Milani (Venice: Corbo e Fiore, 1983); for falsifications (below) see Menegazzo, "Altre osservazioni," 253–61.

26. Quoted in Zorzi, "Note," 1436. The account has bewildered scholars because of the unlikelihood that a theater existed in such a wilderness. To resolve the problem, Zorzi (p. 1437) proposed that the theater is that built by Cornaro in Padua, while Menegazzo ("Ricerche," 201–2) suggested that one had been constructed at Cornaro's villa at Este. The plays could also have been performed in the open air. For Cornaro's success see Lovarini, "Nuovi documenti," in *Studi,* 61–80.

27. Cf. Pullan, *Rich and Poor,* 242–43. For famine victims see Piero Camporesi, *Il pane selvaggio* (Bologna: Il Mulino, 1980), 5–23.

28. Cf. Paul Grendler, *Critics of the Italian World (1530–1560)* (Madison: University of Wisconsin Press, 1969), 15–16; for below see Sambin, "Altre testimonianze," 235–36.

29. See Ginzburg, *Night Battles,* 33–68; for the document below see Menegazzo, "Ricerche," 180–81. Alfred Mortier has asked whether Zaccarotto was actually alive and the depiction of him as dead thus a part of the comedy (*Un Dramaturge populaire de la Renaissance italienne Ruzzante [1502–1542],* 2 vols. [Paris: Peyronnet, 1925–26], 2.278, n. 1). Although many scholars have rejected the notion, it has merit, especially in light of Nale's macabre joke in the *Betia,* and should remain an open question until independent evidence of the date of Zaccarotto's death is obtained.

30. Grabher, *Ruzzante,* 147; Nancy Dersofi, "Ruzante: The Paradox of *Snaturalitè*," *Yearbook of Italian Studies* 1 (1971): 148. For Contarini see Sambin, "Altre testimonianze," 231–32.

31. For manuscripts and early editions of the *First Dialogue* see Zorzi, "Note," 1361, 1615–17, and Giorgio Padoan, "Nota," in *Angelo Beolco Il Ruzante, I Dialoghi, La Seconda Oratione, I Prologhi alla "Moschetta"*, ed. G. Padoan (Padua: Antenore, 1981), 26–28, 30–34. English translations are *Ruzzante Returns from the Wars,* trans. Angela Ingold, *The Gryphon* (Winter 1955): 19–41; *Ruzzante Returns from the Wars,* trans. Angela Ingold and Theodore Hoffman, in *The Classic Theater,* ed. Eric Bentley, 4 vols. (Garden City, N.Y.: Doubleday & Co., 1958), 1.59–77. While the translation has many fine points, it sometimes takes an exaggerated tone that is more appropriate to late than early sixteenth-century theater. Information on the *Second Dialogue* is given in chapter 4, note 45.

32. Lovarini, "Ruzzante a Venezia," 83, "Del tradurre," in *Studi,* 357; Zorzi, "Note," 1362, n. 4, and 1371, n. 55; Padoan, "Guerra," 273.

33. For Agnadello see Francesco Guicciardini, *History of Italy,* trans., ed., with notes and an introduction by Sidney Alexander (Toronto: Macmillan, 1969), book 8, chapter 2. Cremona was retaken for the Venetians by Michael Gaismayr, an event of which Beolco may have been particularly aware because of the Cremonese porter linked to his family (cf. Sambin, "Lazzaro," 179). Ten years later, Gaismayr led a peasant revolt in the Tyrol (Alto Adige); after its failure, he took refuge in Venice and Padua, where he continued to agitate for a peasant insurgence. See Giorgio Padoan, "La dimora padovana di Michele Gaismar e la richiesta di 'Leze e stratuti nuovi,'" in *Momenti,* 239–48, though the trivialization of Beolco's attitudes

toward the peasants is not shared here. See also J. S. Schapiro, *Social Reform and the Reformation,* Studies in History, Economic, and Public Law Edited by the Faculty of Political Science of Columbia University, vol. 34, no. 2 (New York: Columbia University, 1909), esp. 145ff, though Gaismayr's death date is 1532; cf. Padoan, "Dimora," 243.

34. Padoan, "Guerra," 249–73; see esp. 256–57.

35. Grabher, *Ruzzante,* 31–32, 100; cf. Lovarini, *Antichi testi,* 48, and "Introduzione," x–xxix. For army pillaging see Gilbert, *Pope,* 31–32, and Mallett and Hale, *Military Organization,* 352.

36. See chapter 3, note 18.

37. Giuseppe Tassini, *Curiosità veneziane,* 8th ed. (Venice: Filippi, 1970), 231.

38. Particularly important in this, it seems to me, is the pairing of Ruzante and Menato, the stage names by which the two actors would be known even when their roles bore others, and which do not occur together in any surviving early play. That Beolco was willing to rewrite is proven by the revisions to the *Betia* and the *Moscheta.*

39. The name is frequently translated incorrectly as Genevieve or a variation upon it; it is the nickname of Benvegnua, Benvenuta (Welcomed), the irony of which will soon become evident.

40. Bartolomeo d'Alviano, a commander of the Venetian army, fled from defeat by Imperial forces on 7 October 1513; probably caused by his own impetuousness, the defeat was blamed by both Alviano and his funeral orator Andrea Navagero on the cowardice of his troops, a characterization that Beolco seems particularly intent on debunking. For Alviano see Mallett and Hale, *Military Organization,* 288, 295; a synopsis of the wars conducted between 1509 and 1529 is given on pp. 221–27; for military life see pp. 316, 350–54, 494, 500 and J. R. Hale, "The Soldier in German Graphic Art of the Renaissance," *Journal of Interdisciplinary History* 17.1 (1986): 93–94.

41. Cf. Emilio Menegazzo, "Stato economico-sociale del padovano all'epoca del Ruzante," in *La poesia rusticana del Rinascimento,* Accademia dei Lincei, Anno 366, Quaderno 129, (Rome: Accademia dei Lincei, 1969), 162–65.

42. Grabher, *Ruzzante,* 98–121, summarized in the remainder of this paragraph; quoted passage p. 115.

43. Cf. Gaetano Cozzi, "La giustizia e la politica nella Repubblica di Venezia," *Repubblica,* 107–8; Finlay, *Politics,* 196–226.

44. For the clarity with which some writers reflect the attitudes of their times, see Leo Spitzer, "Linguistics and Literary History," in *Linguistics and Literary Style,* ed. Donald Freeman (New York: Holt, Rinehart & Winston, 1970), 25.

45. For early editions and Modenese manuscript, see Zorzi, "Note," 1617–18 (for the Beolco autograph, pp. 1596–97); Padoan, "Nota ai testi," 28–33. English translations include *Bilora,* trans. Babette Hughes and Glenn Hughes, in *World Drama,* ed. Barrett H. Clark, 2 vols. (New York: Dover, 1933), 2.1–9; and *Bilora,* trans. Anthony Caputi, in *Masterworks of World Drama,* ed. A. Caputi, 6 vols. (Bos-

ton: D.C. Heath, 1968), 3.38–47. Both are generally sound translations, although in each case errors detract from the effectiveness of the crucial final scenes; in the Caputi translation, for example (46–47), the final two sentences of Andronico's speech in his dialogue with Pitaro belong to the latter character. The sentence in Bilora's soliloquy reading "The best thing would be to get him outside and settle it here" would better read "It's better for me to get rid of him and get out of here." Similarly, "Now he comes on, and I give it to him—just so I don't kill him" should read "And I'll hit him and give it to him until I've killed him." The chronology preceding the play should also be taken with caution.

46. The deformation of the old man's name, typical of the fate of learned words in the mouths of Beolco's peasants, also foreshadows the plays' ending in its allusion to the verb *andarsene*, "to be on your way," which here is put not in the usual reflexive but given a first person subject, with the meaning thus "I will get you on your way." The above expands upon Caputi, *Bilora*, 39, n. 35.

47. Akin to a bowie knife; see, for example, Pieter Brueghel the Elder, *Peasant Wedding*, in Wolfgang Prohaska, *The Kunsthistorische Museum Vienna: The Paintings Collection* (London: Philip Wilson; Sommerfield, 1984), 61.

48. Nino Borsellino, "Ruzzante," col. 1345 and Guido Davico Bonino, "Introduzione," in *Il teatro italiano: La commedia del Cinquecento*, ed. Guido Davico Bonino, 2 vols. (Turin: Einaudi, 1977), 1.lxii–lxviii, quoted passage p. lxv. For Castegnola as Bilora see Bernardino Scardeone, *De antiquitate urbis Patavii et claris civibus patavini* (Basel, 1560), 255, the only one of Beolco's co-actors whose first name is not given. Less than a year and a half after Beolco's death, his widow married a Zaccaria Castegnola, possibly the same man and certainly a member of the same family (Sambin, "Briciole," 278–84), leaving the critic to wonder if the theme of the girlfriend/wife besieged by the best friend so popular in Beolco's plays was suggested by personal experience. For below see Grendler, *Critics*, 14.

49. Cf. Christopher Robinson, *Lucian and His Influence on Europe* (Chapel Hill: University of North Carolina Press, 1979), 83–84; the plot also resembles that of *Decameron* 2.10 (although there the younger man successfully steals the old man's wife), which Zorzi has connected with *Flora's Play*.

50. Luther Peterson, "Melanchthon on Resisting the Emperor: The *Von der Notwehr Unterricht* of 1547," in *Regno, Religio et Ratio: Essays Presented to Robert M. Kingdon*, ed. Jerome Friedman, Sixteenth Century Essays and Studies, vol. 8 (Kirksville, Mo.: Sixteenth Century Journal Publishers, 1987), 133–44; quoted passage p. 140.

51. For biography see Sambin, "Altre testimonianze," 244, document 5.

52. See, for example, Cozzi, "Authority and the Law in Renaissance Venice," in *Renaissance Venice*, esp. 296–97; Finlay, *Politics*, 163–226, esp. 182; Ugo Tucci, "Psychology," 346–78.

53. Jacob Burckhardt, *The Civilization of the Renaissance*, trans. S. G. C. Middlemore, 2 vols. (New York: Harper and Brothers, 1929); and see William J. Bouwsma, "The Renaissance and the Drama of Western History," *American Histor-*

ical Review 84 (1979): 1–15. Growing numbers of cultural historians are reviewing the Burckhardt thesis with at least qualified favor.

Chapter Five

1. See chapter 4 and *Moscheta* (*RT,* 687), "if I too wanted to speak in Florentine and *moscheto . . .* I would have flies."

2. Padoan, "Angelo," 159–64. While the *Moscheta* may have been completed after *Flora's Play,* it is discussed here because the bulk of the material is earlier. Dovehouse Books, Toronto, has announced an English translation by Ronald Ferguson and Antonio Franceschetti in its Carleton Renaissance Plays in Translation series.

3. Baratto, "L'esordio," 66, n. 95, attributed to the falseness of the city that drives people apart.

4. Soldiers were billeted with the local population.

5. Possibly a reference to the powerful Council of Ten: cf. Guido Ruggiero, *Violence in Early Renaissance Venice* (New Brunswick, N.J.: Rutgers University Press, 1980), 6–17; Mallett and Hale, *Military Organization,* 249ff. The number of men Ruzante will take out (below) may include Andronico and Tonin, an intertextual allusion permitted by the constancy and intimacy of Beolco's audiences.

6. Sentences in square brackets are stage directions added by Zorzi; Ruzante uses the same verb for the murders and the sexual conquest, fruits of a single aggressive instinct.

7. Padoan has pointed out the similarity to Ariosto's *Orlando furioso* 43.31ff: "Angelo," 164, n. 218; the plan also seems linked with the medieval topos of the husband who tests his wife's fidelity; cf. Boccaccio, *Decameron,* 7.5, in which a man dresses as a priest to hear his wife's confession.

8. Cf. Menegazzo, "Stato," 155, n. 40.

9. Indicating that Beolco viewed illegitimacy as shameful. The insult "marten" links Ruzante with Weasel, as the two animals are closely related.

10. Giovanni Della Casa, *Galateo,* trans. with an introduction and notes by Konrad Eisenbichler and Kenneth R. Bartlett (Toronto: Center for Reformation and Renaissance Studies, 1986); biographical information from the introduction.

11. Nino Borsellino, *Gli anticlassicisti del Cinquecento* (Rome-Bari: Laterza, 1973); following material summarizes Guido Davico Bonino, *Lo scrittore, il potere, la maschera* (Padua: Liviana, 1979).

12. Pullan, *Rich and Poor,* 373 and passim.

13. Elaine Pagels, *Adam, Eve, and the Serpent* (New York: Random House, 1988); this paragraph summarizes the excerpt "The Politics of Paradise," *New York Review of Books* 35.8 (1988): 28–37.

14. For Augustine and Luther see Steven Ozment, *The Age of Reform: An Intellectual and Religious History of Late Medieval and Reformation Europe* (New Haven: Yale University Press, 1980), 22–30, 44–72, 231–89; see also Peterson, "Melanchthon."

15. Prosperi, *Angelo Beolco,* 94–97.

16. See, for example, Zorzi, "Note," 1399; Padoan, "Angelo," 160; as will be shown below, Alvarotto's role virtually disappears from Beolco's subsequent plays, indicating that the breach was not permanently healed.

17. If the playwright's early demise resulted from malaria caught while working for Cornaro in the swampy lower Po Valley (Menegazzo, "Stato," 147), he may have already been ill.

18. For classical conformity see Padoan, "Angelo," 163–64.

19. Lovarini, "Prologhi," 340; Padoan, "Angelo," 148–49, and "Fiorina," 55 and n. 1; Maganza, "Al clarissimo Cavalier," 1.296: "I know that Padua would never have heard him [Beolco] / sing as we do / and his beautiful Tresa and the *Fiorina* / would never have passed Lezzafusina"; cf. chapter 3, n. 18.

20. Earlier, such appeals had been limited to a brief, formulaic request at the end of the prologue; their elaboration follows Beolco's formation of a (semi) professional troupe, and is accompanied by other comments that reveal an awareness of its members' views, perhaps prompted by the difficulty of recruiting sufficient actors: cf. Beolco's letter to Ercole II, *RT,* 1253.

21. Also "to groom" or "to harness," as in the *Moscheta;* for diminished obscenity (below) see Padoan, "Angelo," 153–57.

22. A clever way of avoiding that traditional obligation, to which Beolco had objected in the prologue of the *Betia* (*RT,* 155).

23. Cf. Ginzburg, *Night Battles,* chapter 2.

24. The plot develops a line of Ruzante's in the *Moscheta* (*RT,* 609). Bedon's cameo part seems to have been Alvarotto's role.

25. See, for example, Grabher, *Ruzzante,* 174–82. Padoan, "Fiorina," has influenced the discussion below; if the figure of the woman stands metaphorically for Beolco's inheritance, an earlier version, which Padoan considers a possibility, could correlate with Angelo's intention to claim a share by force, one which the legal documents bear out. The losing suitor's name is the dialect version of Melchiorre (one which, to my knowledge, does not occur in other contemporary theatrical texts), perhaps implying that Angelo was determined not to suffer the exclusion that his uncle had.

26. Such a deus ex machina ending, as Professor Thomas Fay observed in an insightful lecture on Mozart's *Don Giovanni* sponsored by the Department of French and Italian of Tulane University, was a form of literary repressiveness that paralleled the political repressiveness of the ancien régime.

27. Lovarini, "Prologhi," 337.

28. Terence Murphy, "'Woful Childe of Parents Rage': Suicide of Children and Adolescents in Early Modern England, 1507–1710," *Sixteenth Century Journal* 17 (1986): 259.

29. I am comforted in this analysis by the similar findings of scholars of Spanish theater: see Div. on Subversion behind the Multiple Masks of the Comic Muse, MLA Convention, 29 December 1988.

Chapter Six

1. Preliminary material for both plays is presented here; Beolco's petition is reprinted in Zorzi, "Note," 1515; Lovarini, "Per l'edizione," 161–62 and see pp. 145–47 for Marciana manuscript. For device see J. P. Tomasini, *Illustrium virorum elogia* (Padua, 1630), 35, tav. 3, reproduced in Lovarini, opposite p. 17. For performance see Sanuto, *Diarii,* vol. 57, cols. 528, 549; Beolco, "Letter to Duke Ercole d'Este," *RT,* 1253; Padoan, "Angelo," 164–66; Zorzi, "Note," 1482–83. For comparisons with Plautine texts, which Beolco may have known through Renaissance translations rather than in the original, and which he adapted to his own values, see Oliveira Barata, "Sulla cultura," 115–37; Mario Baratto, "'Pavano' e 'latino': la *Piovana* e il problema dell'imitazione," in *Convegno internazionale,* 129–47; Roberto Alonge, "Ritorno a casa: Angelo Beolco da Ruzante a Plauto," in *Convegno internazionale,* 93–104.

2. Paolo Sambin, "Gli studenti giuristi, Alvise Cornaro (e il Ruzante), Pietro Bembo," in *Convegno internazionale,* 181–87.

3. Douglas Radcliff-Umstead notes the same image in the prologue of Machiavelli's *Clizia;* see *The Birth of Modern Comedy in the Renaissance* (Chicago: University of Chicago Press, 1969), 219. Machiavelli's play, performed in 1525 (Silvia Ruffo-Fiore, *Niccolò Machiavelli* [Boston: Twayne, 1982], 116) may have been known to Beolco through theatrical contacts or through Florentine Republican exiles.

4. Like other parts of the prologue, reminiscent of the prologue of Bibbiena's *Calandria:* Padoan, "L'*Anconitana* tra Boccaccio, Bibbiena e Ariosto," in *Momenti,* 278.

5. The passage demonstrates the author's positing of precise experience as the substratum of literary metaphors.

6. A self-protective word game typical of the late plays; both Catos stood for the values of the Roman republic, the younger committing suicide when hopes for the preservation of the free state ended with Caesar's victory.

7. A possible reference to Bembo; cf. *Betia, RT,* 179, and Fido, "Introduction," 206.

8. Piove was the site of some Lutheran conversions: cf. John Martin, "The Sect of Benedetto Corazzaro," 2. It should be noted that at the time "Lutheran" was frequently a vague term applied to anyone at variance with orthodox Catholicism.

9. A typical situation: cf. Guido Ruggiero, *The Boundaries of Eros* (New York and Oxford: Oxford University Press, 1985), 28–30 and passim. For the return of the dowry (below) see pp. 25, 30–31.

10. As Fernanda Vitali noted, the master in the Plautine play gives most of the treasure back to the pimp, retaining a sum to free his slave ("La *Piovana* di Ruzzante e la *Rudens* di Plauto," *Bollettino del Museo Civico di Padova* 45 [1956]: 27–28). There are hints, however, that he will actually keep the money for himself, a short-changing of the servant that Beolco has developed more subtly here in the question of shared rights and rewards; in 1530, in the town of Este where Cornaro had a villa, a

Roman vase filled with silver and gold coins and other precious objects was found by a peasant. The Venetian state determined that one third belong to it, one third to the Venetian magistrate, and one third to the landlord and finder. The magistrate bought the landlord's third and turned a handsome profit (Sanuto, *Diarii,* vol. 53, col. 261).

11. See Nino Borsellino, "Per Ruzante," in *Rozzi e Intronati: Esperienze e forme di teatro dal "Decameron" al "Candelaio,"* 2d ed. (Rome: Bulzoni, 1976), 178 and Baratto, "'Pavano.'" On literary fame see William Kerrigan, "What Was Donne Doing?" *South Central Review* 4.2 (1987): 11. Roberto Alonge has noted an intense preoccupation with death in Beolco's works, especially *The Girl from Piove* ("Ritorno").

12. Beolco's senate petition indicates that he played Garbinello; the similarity of names and the fact that the pair never occur in the same scene suggest that he played Garbugio as well.

13. For Plautine sources see Radcliff-Umstead, *Birth,* 219–23; Zorzi's meticulous notes; A. Böhm, "Fonti plautine del Ruzzante," *Giornale storico della letteratura italiana* 29.1 (1896): 101–11; and Vitali, "La *Piovana,*" 3–42. Their conclusions must be reevaluated in light of Oliveira Barata's later finding that Beolco relied on a Renaissance translation for *The Cow Comedy.* For Ariosto's *Cassaria* (rewritten in 1529 and performed at Ferrara in 1531 and 1532) see Padoan, "L'*Anconitana,*" 278–80. Beolco also influenced Ariosto's *Lena* (cf. Casella, "Presentazione," xii–xiii). For *Stephanium* see *Il teatro umanistico veneto: la commedia,* ed. Graziana Gentilini (Ravenna: Longo, 1983), 71–74; cf. *Stephanium,* 4.1, 5.4, and 5.5, with *The Girl from Piove,* 5.8, 5.10, and 5.4; Grabher, *Ruzzante,* 223–34.

14. Cf. Menegazzo, "Ricerche," 180, 182, 186, 214; Zorzi, "Note," 1487, n. 13.

15. For Boccaccio borrowing see Zorzi, "Note," 1492–93, n. 43; for the *Decameron* as theatrical sourcebook see Nino Borsellino, "*Decameron* come teatro," *Rozzi,* 11–50; for structures as tools of action for the displaced see Michel de Certeau, *The Practice of Everyday Life,* trans. Steven F. Rendall (Berkeley and Los Angeles: University of California Press, 1984); for below cf. p. 4 on the substitution of God by common man (which Beolco anticipates); for class mores see Carroll, "Who's on Top?"; cf. Ruggiero, *Boundaries,* 29–31, and see in general Diane Owen Hughes, "Urban Growth and Family Structure in Medieval Genoa," *Past and Present* 66 (1975): 3–28.

16. Apparently both a paraphrase of Bibbiena's prologue and a reference to Ariosto, who had recently rewritten his early comedies in verse, refining the language.

17. It was believed that spirits could suck the lifebreath out of sleeping humans; for risers (below), see Zorzi, "Note," 1522–23, n. 16.

18. As Menegazzo notes, all of these problems are dealt with in the play ("Il ruzantiano 'conte Pandin'," in *Medioevo e Rinascimento Veneto con altri studi in onore di Lino Lazzarino,* 2 vols. [Padua: Antenore, 1979], 2.83–134). Each solution is

fanciful, like those of the play's conclusion. In real life, on the other hand, the consequences are serious: Beolco was pursued for debts (Sambin, "Altre testimonianze," 223–26); Conte Pandin, a mad beggar, was made a pretext for invalidating his daughter's presumed marriage to Antonio Barbo; it is almost impossible to ignore an unpleasant spouse. Given this framework, the play's reference to Pandin may not be mocking him (as Menegazzo characterized it), but underlining the fantastical, childlike nature of the comedy's solutions as the only means of avoiding the new social rigidity.

19. Allusions to coitus interruptus and to anal intercourse in Beolco's late prologues and those of other contemporary plays (Ariosto's *Lena,* for example) may indicate that such processes were being used as forms of birth control, the need for which is recognized in the *Second Oration.*

20. *Animalet* puns on *amulet* and *little animal*: Zorzi, "Note," 1524, n. 20; the attaching of pendants to the waists of women's dresses was the latest fashion: cf. Titian, *Portrait of Eleanora Gonzaga* (1536–37; Florence, Uffizi), in *Uffizi Florence,* ed. Carlo Ludovico Ragghianti (New York: Newsweek; Milan: Mondadori, 1968), 103. Gonzaga was wife of Francesco Maria della Rovere. For erotic themes in decorative objects cf. Workshop of Riccio, *Acrobatic lamp* (Modena, Galleria Estense), in *From Borso to Cesare d'Este: An Exhibition in Aid of the Courtauld Institute of Art Trust Appeal June 1st to August 14 1984,* [ed. Peter Matthiesen], 3d ed. (London: Matthiesen Fine Arts in Association with Stair, Sainty, Matthiesen, 1984), cat. 90 and p. 136.

21. As in the 1525 rehearsal, Beolco is insulting the women of the audience: "cow" is a slang term for a woman of low morals (see *RT,* 1105–7). For the *cortegiana onesta* (refined courtesan), of whose increasing influence in the late sixteenth century Fiorninetta is a harbinger, see in general Fiora Bassanese, *Gaspara Stampa* (Boston: Twayne, 1982), esp. 27–29; it was not unusual for such women to be introduced into the profession by their (adoptive) mothers.

22. An impoverished black flambeau carrier for the costly New Orleans Carnival parades affirmed with similar pride: "They cannot perform without us. We is they light" (Michael Smallwood, quoted in Bill Grady, "Flambeaux: The struggle to carry the torch," *New Orleans Times Picayune* 1 March 1987, B4). When clientelism can no longer be enforced, change begins with its rejection (cf. Oliver Sacks, "The Revolution of the Deaf," *New York Review of Books* 35.9 (1988), esp. 28).

23. A literal variation on the Carnival custom of burning the old woman who personifies Lenten deprivation; cf. Toschi, *Le origini,* 139–49; the episode does not occur in Beolco's source.

24. As Placido, the senior man in the play's family, is still alive, this comment seems rooted in Beolco's experience in administering the Beolco patrimony; he would eventually become the formal steward for all of his halfbrothers (Lovarini, "Notizie," 20–25), apparently a function he was already fulfilling informally.

25. For the theatrical tradition of the madam, see Radcliff-Umstead, *Birth,* 225, 40–42, 96–103.

26. Cf. Ruggiero, *Boundaries*, 30–31, for a similar episode involving Geronimo Zorzi, a tale that Beolco could have heard from Domenego Zorzi, a member of the Company of the Farmers and "lord of the party" at his 1524 performance (cf. Sanuto, *Diarii*, vol. 35, cols. 392–93). The protagonist of Beolco's story is Trese; thus the reference to Trese in Magagnò ("Al clarissimo Cavalier," 296) could either be to this play or to a lost one that develops this episode.

27. I.e., unable to act without paternal consent; cf. Thomas Kuehn, *Emancipation in Late Medieval Florence* (New Brunswick, N.J.: Rutgers University Press, 1982).

28. On sycophants see Grendler, *Critics*, 83–84. This scene seems to reflect Beolco's unease and even shame at his role in the Cornaro and Este circles.

29. For Beolco's familiarity with contracts see Lovarini, "Nuovi documenti," 64–66; Sambin, "Lazzaro," documents 1 and 7.

30. The ending derives from the Renaissance translation that Beolco used as his source (Oliveira Barata, "Sulla cultura," 115–37). In light of Oliveira Barata's findings, earlier work on classical sources (Radcliff-Umstead, *Birth*, 224–27; Zorzi, "Note"; Padoan, "Angelo," 168, and "L'*Anconitana*," 277) should be taken with caution. Beolco's decision not to show the conversion on stage seems to indicate that he found it too contrived. The stalk metaphor (below), indiscriminately mixing positive and negative leaves, seems peculiarly out of tune with Beolco's belief in natural motivations; Nancy Dersofi (*Arcadia and the Stage* [Madrid: Porrua; Washington, D.C.: Studia Humanitatis, 1978], 144) views it as a symbol of mutability that produces constancy.

31. Convents for reformed prostitutes, which first arose in the years Celega refers to (another example of Beolco's strong need to be at the forefront of cultural trends). At the date of the play, there was such a convent in Venice but not in Padua, although its bishop Cardinal Francesco Pisani (at least later) would become involved in the movement. For this and poor girls drawn into prostitution see Pullan, *Rich and Poor*, 375–94. For the chaste prostitute see Louise George Clubb, "La commedia grave del XVI secolo all'estero," in *Interrogative dell'Umanesimo,* ed. Giovannangiola Tarugi, 3 vols. (Florence: Olschki, 1976), 1.151. *The Cow Comedy* seems to develop out of Garbinello's instruction to Resca in *The Girl from Piove* that she pretend that Nina is a child she found during the war and raised; the connection is reciprocated with Celega's praise for Nina.

32. Cf. Chojnacki, "La posizione," esp. 69–70; for damage to conjugal bond see Diane Owen Hughes, "From Brideprice to Dowry in Mediterranean Europe," *Women and History* 10 (1985): 13–58; for obsession with money see Cozzi, "Authority," 331ff.

33. Grabher, *Ruzzante,* 210–15.

34. *Liminic* is introduced here to bridge the terms *liminal* and *liminoid* (i.e., referring to that cluster of activities regardless of its role in society).

Chapter Seven

1. See Zorzi, "Nota al testo," 1621, n. 8; for performances see Padoan, "Angelo," 176–77. The Venetian performance could have occurred earlier in Beolco's career. See also Radcliff-Umstead, *Birth,* 214–19.

2. For dating, see Mortier, *Dramaturge,* 1.141–44; Lovarini, "La *Pastorale,*" 289–90; Zorzi, "Nota," in Ruzante, *Anconitana* (Padua: Randi, 1953), 183–92; Grabher, "Sulla datazione dell'*Anconitana,*" *La Rassegna della letteratura italiana* s. 7, 58 (1954): 62–68; Borsellino, "Per Ruzante," 161–85; Padoan, "Angelo," 171–81; Zorzi, "Note," 1459–60.

3. See, for example, Giovanni Mansueti, *Healing of the Daughter of Ser Nicolò Benvegnudo of San Polo* (Venice, Accademia), in Patricia Fortini Brown, *Venetian Narrative Painting in the Age of Carpaccio* (New Haven: Yale University Press, 1988), plate 23. For later fashions see Lorenzo Lotto, *Gentleman in His Study* (Venice, Accademia), in *L'opera completa del Lotto,* ed. Rodolfo Pallucchini and G. Mariani Canova (Milan: Rizzoli, 1975), plate 48. For earrings see Gentile Bellini, *Miracle at the Bridge of San Lorenzo* (Venice, Accademia), in Brown, plate 20.

4. Cf. Mario Baratto, "Da Ruzante al Beolco," in *Poesia rusticana,* 109.

5. Beolco seems to co-opt Bembo's atypical Carnival *Stanze* celebrating carnal love, performed in 1507 and printed in 1530 and 1535. Cf. *Prose e Rime,* 651–71; for dates see Dionisotti, "Nota biografica," 58–59. Similar views are also expressed by the less-than-Platonic Gismondo in the *Asolani,* book 2, chapters 19–20 (cf. Padoan, "Angelo," 185), printed in 1505 and 1530. Bembo moved to Padua in 1522, a fact that may point to an early version of the play.

6. A play on the Latin *comedere,* "to eat."

7. Apparently unaware that Doralice is standing at the window to advertise her own services; her line of work and tryst with the married Tomao render her praise of the youths' virtues and advocacy of women's use of cosmetics to keep their husbands from other women (below) ironic.

8. The vogue for cosmetics is an aspect of Renaissance narcissism noted by Davico Bonino (cf. "Narcisismo e alienazione nella *Vita* del Cellini," *Lo scrittore,* 41–58) and condemnation of it was common at the time (cf. Erasmus, *Praise of Folly,* 111; Bibbiena, *Calandria,* 5.3). The elaborate formula for perfume may have come from Beolco's cousin, a compounder of scents, for whom see Lovarini, "Notizie," 9–10.

9. A metaphor whose only other occurrence is in *The Cow Comedy,* 1157.

10. Lovarini's fundamental article, "Le canzoni popolari in Ruzante e in altri scrittori alla pavana del secolo XVI," in *Studi,* 165–99, lists no other instance of these (185).

11. A typically Paduan name, derived from the saint believed to have been the first bishop of the city.

12. A counterpoint to Leone Ebreo's popular summary of Neoplatonic theory; first printed in 1535, it was begun early in the century and could have been known to Beolco through Leone's links with Venice or through the connection of

both with the medical profession; cf. *Dialoghi d'amore,* ed. Santino Caramella (Bari: Laterza, 1929), 136, 222, and "Nota," 419–24; *Betia, RT,* 173. For the work's influence see Ettore Bonora, "Il Classicismo dal Bembo al Guarini," in *Storia della letteratura italiana,* 9 vols. (Milan: Garzanti, 1965–69), 4.232–34. The mockery of love recalls the attitude of Bazarelo in the *Betia.*

13. An image that will occur in Beolco's last work, the *Letter to Alvarotto, RT,* 1235.

14. Dersofi ("Ruzante," 155) stresses the connection here between song and harmony.

15. A sword was a sign of gentlemanly status; when Ruzante was poor he carried a knife.

16. See also Gianfranco De Bosio, "Un trentennio di lavoro sul Ruzante e Ludovico Zorzi," in *Convengo internazionale,* 244.

17. Documentation in Padoan, "Angelo," 181–89, and "L'*Anconitana,*" 280–83; interpretation inspired by Borsellino, "Ruzzante," col. 1344 and Grabher, *Ruzzante,* 192–93. For the following considerations see Carroll, "Who's on Top?"

18. Padoan, "Angelo," 189; Boccaccio, *Comedia Ninfe* 3.8.

19. Cf. Padoan, "Angelo," 189, n. 297; Angelico Prati, *Etimologie venete,* ed. Gianfranco Folena and Giambattista Pellegrini (Venice-Rome: Istituto per la Collaborazione Culturale, 1968), s.v.; Ottorino Pianigiani, *Vocabolario etimologico della lingua italiana* (Milan: Sonzogno, 1943), s.v.

20. Grabher, *Ruzzante,* 201.

21. Zorzi, "Note," 1582; for manuscripts see "Nota al testo," 1630.

22. Zorzi has identified the cultural traditions that Beolco passes in review: Lady Sophrosina represents classical philosophy; Lady Temperance, Alvise Cornaro's sober life; and the three followers, Elias, Enoch, and John the Divine ("Note," 1585, notes 3, 4, and 5).

23. A pun on *vita* (life) and *vite* (screw).

24. It was a common belief that the soul left the body during sleep (Ginzburg, *Night Battles,* 8, 10, 19, and passim). Fido has noted that Beolco's career both began and ended with a dream ("Introduction," 213).

25. Puns upon *vita* (life) and *vite* (vine).

26. The personifications of inanimate objects here are the culmination of a trend that began in *The Veteran:* cf. Grabher, *Ruzzante,* 105–6.

27. Two parts of the Roman Catholic mass that are often sung.

28. Grabher, *Ruzzante,* 249; cf. Borsellino's sage comment that the conflict between various forces in Beolco's work reached a crisis after which it was no longer possible for him to write ("Per Ruzante," 185).

29. Cf. Dante Alighieri, *Divine Comedy, Paradise,* xxxii–xxxiii.

30. A portion of this sentence paraphrases Michel de Certeau's characterization of Freudian analysis (*Practice,* 4).

31. Marisa Milani, "*Snaturalité* e deformazione nella lingua teatrale del Ruzzante," *Quaderni del Circolo Filologico Linguistico Padovano* 2 (1970): 122.

Chapter Eight

1. See Nicola Savarese, "In morte di Angelo Beolco detto Ruzante. La *Canace* dello Speroni," *Biblioteca teatrale* 15–16 (1976): 170–90; Sperone Speroni, *Canace e Scritti in sua difesa;* Giambattista Giraldi Cinzio, *Scritti contro la Canace: Giudizio ed Epistola latina* (Bologna: Commissione per i testi di lingua, 1982). Speroni was the son of Bernardino Speroni, an executor of Beolco's father's will (Lovarini, "Notizie," 20).

2. For crisis see Borsellino, "Per Ruzante," 177–85; for land management see Lovarini, "Nuovi documenti," 61–81. Beolco also assumed much of the direction of the family patrimony because one of his halfbrothers was in exile, one was in prison, and one was a minor (Lovarini, "Notizie," 20–33). Through his activities and Speroni's writings he became embroiled posthumously in an accusation of usury (Lovarini, "Notizie," 33ff, and Menegazzo, "Ricerche," 212–13).

3. Lovarini, "Per l'edizione," 115–119; for Calmo in general see *Le lettere di Andrea Calmo,* ed. Vittorio Rossi (Turin: Loescher, 1888), esp. the important "Introduzione."

4. For the group and their works see Lovarini, "Per l'edizione," 121–25; id., "Le canzoni," 190–99, and Mortier, *Dramaturge,* 1.181–95. For below see Sperone Speroni, *Dialogo delle lingue e Dialogo della rettorica,* ed. Giuseppe DeRobertis (Lanciano: Carabba, 1912). For the *questione della lingua* see the important monograph by Robert A. Hall, Jr., *The Italian Questione della Lingua* (Chapel Hill: University of North Carolina Press, 1942), esp. 13–18.

5. For editions see Zorzi, "Nota al testo," 1604–32 (for Maganza, 1609); Lovarini, "Per l'edizione," 129–33; Mortier, *Dramaturge,* 260–76.

6. Stillman Drake, *Galileo* (Oxford: Oxford University Press, 1980), 39; Galileo Galilei, *Galileo against the Philosophers in His Dialogue of Cecco di Ronchitti (1605) and Considerations of Alimberto Mauri (1606),* trans. Stillman Drake (Los Angeles: Zeitlin and Ver Brugge, 1976).

7. Louis Riccoboni, *Histoire du théâtre italien* (1730; Turin: Bottega d'Erasmo, 1968), 50–56, 133–34; cf. Francesco S. Quadrio, *Storia e ragione d'ogni poesia* (Milan, 1744), 3.2, 227, and Giovanni Maria Mazzuchelli, *Gli scrittori d'Italia* (Brescia, 1760), 2.5. 908. I am grateful to Professor Harry Redman, Jr., for various facts concerning the rediscovery of Beolco by the Romantics. For below see Maurice Sand, *Masques et buffons,* 2 vols. (Paris, 1862), 2.77–118; translated as *The History of the Harlequinade,* 2 vols. (London: Secker, 1915), 1.279–311.

8. Lovarini, "Premesse alle traduzioni," in *Studi* 360; Gay Manifold, *George Sand's Theatrical Career* (Ann Arbor, Mich.: UMI Research Press, 1985), 135–39, 148–50; Harry Redman, Jr., personal communication.

9. Lovarini's career and its intellectual context are superbly evoked by Gianfranco Folena in "La vita e gli studi di Emilio Lovarini," in *Studi,* followed by a complete annotated bibliography, vii–lxxvii; see also "Per l'edizione," 133–37; Winifred Smith, *The Commedia dell'Arte* (1912; New York: Blom, 1964), 52–57;

Kathleen M. Lea, *Italian Popular Comedy* (1934; New York: Russell and Russell, 1962), 233–38. The latter is more reliable.

10. See Lovarini, "Del tradurre Ruzzante," in *Studi*, 346, 349–350, and "Premesse," 360–61; Nicola Mangini, "Il Ruzante di Cesco Baseggio," in *Convegno internazionale*, 211–19.

11. See De Bosio, "Un trentennio di lavoro sul Ruzante e Ludovico Zorzi" and "Un trentennio di lavoro sul Ruzante" in *Convegno internazionale*, 221–36.

12. Heinz Riedt, "Cenni su una integrale transponibilità della poetica ruzantiana in lingua tedesca," in *Convegno internazionale*, 203–4; Margo Berthold, "La conoscenza del Ruzante in Germania attraverso gli spettacoli dopo il 1945," in *Convegno internazionale*, 205–9; Giacomo Oreglia, "La Casa Editrice 'Italia' e la diffusione dell'opera di Ruzante all'estero," in *Convegno internazionale*, 201–2.

13. See Zorzi, "Nota al testo," 1617–26 (concluding remarks to each play).

14. Calendoli, *Ruzante*, 167–73.

15. Beyond the material contained in the present study, see Sambin, "Gli studenti giuristi," 183.

16. Michael Bertin, "Introduction," in *The Play and Its Critic: Essays for Eric Bentley*, ed. M. Bertin (Lanham, Md.: University Press of America, 1986), xv.

Selected Bibliography

PRIMARY WORKS

Italian Editions

I Dialoghi, La Seconda Oratione, I Prologhi alla Moschetta. Edited by Giorgio Padoan. Padua: Antenore, 1981.
Moschetta, Fiorina. Edited by Emilio Lovarini. Rome: Edizioni Italiane, 1941.
La pastoral, La Prima Oratione, Una Lettera giocosa. Edited by Giorgio Padoan. Padua: Antenore, 1978.
La Pastorale. Edited by Emilio Lovarini. Florence: La Nuova Italia, 1951.
Il reduce, Bilora, Menego. Edited by Emilio Lovarini. Rome: Edizioni Universitarie, 1940.
Ruzante Teatro. Edited by Ludovico Zorzi. Turin: Einaudi, 1967.

English Translations

Bilora. Translated by Babette and Glenn Hughes. In *World Drama*, edited by Barrett H. Clark. Vol. 1. New York: Dover, 1933. A generally sound translation but with some errors.
Bilora. Translated by Anthony Caputi. In *Masterworks of World Drama*, edited by Anthony Caputi. Vol. 3. Boston: D.C. Heath, 1968. A generally sound translation but with some errors. Biography dated.
Ruzzante Returns from the Wars. Translated by Angela Ingold and Theodore Hoffman. In *The Classic Theater,* edited by Eric Bentley. Vol. 1. Garden City, N.Y.: Doubleday, 1958. A good translation, though the tone is a bit exaggerated at times.

SECONDARY WORKS

Alonge, Roberto. "Ritorno a casa: Angelo Beolco da Ruzante a Plauto." In *Convegno internazionale di Studi sul Ruzante,* edited by Giovanni Calendoli and Giuseppe Vellucci, 93–104. Venice: Corbo e Fiore, 1987. Detailed comparison of *The Girl from Piove* and Plautus's *Rope,* showing how Beolco adapted his source to his theatrical values.
Baratto, Mario. "L'esordio di Ruzante." In *Tre studi sul teatro.* Venice: Neri Pozza,

1968. Discusses Beolco's sympathy for peasants and antipathy for literary world. Locates Beolco in theatrical, historical, and cultural contexts.

————. "'Pavano' e 'latino': la *Piovana* e il problema dell'imitazione." In *Convegno internazionale di Studi sul Ruzante*, edited by Giovanni Calendoli and Giuseppe Vellucci, 129–47. Venice: Corbo e Fiore, 1987. Sees Beolco's Plautine plays as revivals of his polemic stimulated by personal crisis; underlines the importance of realism in *The Girl from Piove*.

Borsellino, Nino. "Ruzzante." *Enciclopedia dello Spettacolo,* vol. 8; cols. 1342–49. Roma: Le Maschere, 1954–68. Demonstrates that Beolco's loyalty to peasants underlies his satire of learned culture.

————. "Per Ruzante." In *Rozzi e Intronati: Esperienze e forme di teatro dal "Decameron" al "Candelaio."* Rome: Bulzoni, 1976. Sees Beolco as moving away from formal literature toward realism; find understanding of Beolco's concerns.

Calendoli, Giovanni. *Ruzante.* Venice: Corbo e Fiore, 1985. Examines connection between Beolco's espousal of peasants and Cornaro's agrarian policy. Valuable insights into theatrical methods.

————. "Le immagini di Venezia sul primo teatro di Angelo Beolco." In *Convegno internazionale di Studi sul Ruzante,* edited by Giovanni Calendoli and Giuseppe Vellucci, 263–73. Venice: Corbo e Fiore, 1987. Holds that it was Beolco's emphasis upon the importance and autonomy of Padua (within an idealized vision of an eclectic Venetian republic) that scandalized Venetian officials in 1523.

Calendoli, Giovanni, and Giuseppe Velucci, eds., *Convegno internazionale di Studi sul Ruzante.* Venice: Corbo e Fiore, 1987. Proceedings of a wide-ranging and richly informative conference held in 1983.

Carroll, Linda. "Carnival Rites as Vehicles of Protest in Renaissance Venice." *Sixteenth Century Journal* 16 (1985): 487–502. Locates Beolco's plays in their Carnival context; explores social and personal roots of protest.

————. "Authorial Defense in Boccaccio and Ruzante: From Liminal to Liminoid." *Romance Quarterly* 34 (1987): 103–16. Delineates cultural shift between Middle Ages and Renaissance in which Beolco participated; offers biographical interpretation of Beolco's polemic.

————. "Ruzante's Early Adaptations from More and Erasmus." *Italica* 66 (1989): 29–34. Analyzes how Beolco adapted ideas from More and Erasmus to bolster radical social reform.

De Bosio, Gianfranco. "Un trentennio di lavoro sul Ruzante." In *Convegno internazionale di Studi sul Ruzante,* edited by Giovanni Calendoli and Giuseppe Vellucci, 221–36. Venice: Corbo e Fiore, 1987. Eloquent evocation of the work of the author, Ludovico Zorzi, and others to bring Beolco's texts before the postwar Italian public, both in print and on stage.

Dersofi, Nancy. *Arcadia and the Stage.* Madrid: Porrua; Washington, D.C.: Studia Humanitatis, 1978. First monograph in English on Beolco; gives basic scholarship, plot summaries; translates some passages; sees Beolco as using theater to create a perfected version of peasant world.

————. "Ruzante: the Paradox of *Snaturalité*." *Yearbook of Italian Studies* 1 (1971): 142–55. Stresses role of music and theatrical tropes in plays.

Fantazzi, Charles E. "Ruzzante's Rustic Challenge to Arcadia." *Studies in Philology* 82 (1985): 81–103. Discusses Arcadian background of the *Pastoral*.

Ferguson, Ronald. "Moralità convenzionale e moralità naturale in tre commedie del Ruzante." In *Convegno internazionale di Studi sul Ruzante*, edited by Giovanni Calendoli and Giuseppe Vellucci, 21–35. Venice: Corbo e Fiore, 1987. Demonstrates that Beolco's ethical system is based on natural drives rather than Christian ideals.

Fido, Franco. "An Introduction to the Theater of Angelo Beolco." *Renaissance Drama* 6 (1973): 203–18. Excellent introduction; balanced discussion of scholarship; new insights.

————. "La lettera a Marco Alvarotto e le utopie cinquecentesche della vita felice." In *Convegno internazionale di Studi sul Ruzante*, edited by Giovanni Calendoli and Giuseppe Vellucci, 251–62. Venice: Corbo e Fiore, 1987. Compares the *Letter* to other Renaissance utopias. Stresses moderation of emotions.

Grabher, Carlo. *Ruzzante*. Milan-Messina: Principato, 1953. Basic monograph that explicates plays, explores their sympathy for common people, and applauds their innovative spirit.

Herrick, Marvin. *Italian Comedy in the Renaissance*. Urbana: University of Illinois Press, 1960. Section on Beolco sympathetically discusses peasant plays.

Lovarini, Emilio. *Studi sul Ruzzante e sulla letteratura pavana*. Edited by Gianfranco Folena. Padua: Antenore, 1965. Path-breaking work based on archival and manuscript materials. Reconstruction of biography and sociocultural context of works.

Menegazzo, Emilio. "Stato economico-sociale del padovano all'epoca del Ruzante." *La poesia rusticana nel Rinascimento*. Rome: Accademia dei Lincei, 1969. Finds that Beolco's portrait of peasant life was fundamentally accurate; important additions to biographical information.

Menegazzo, Emilio, and Paolo Sambin. "Nuove esplorazioni archivistiche per Angelo Beolco e Alvise Cornaro." 1: Sambin, "Lazzaro e Giovanni Francesco Beolco, nonno e padre del Ruzante." 2: Menegazzo, "Ricerche intorno alla vita e all'ambiente del Ruzante e di Alvise Cornaro." 3: Sambin, "Altre testimonianze (1525–1540) di Angelo Beolco." *Italia Medioevale e Umanistica* 7 (1964): 133–247. 4: Menegazzo, "Altre osservazioni intorno alla vita e all'ambiente del Ruzante e di Alvise Cornaro." 5: Sambin, "Briciole biografiche del Ruzante e del suo compagno d'arte Marco Aurelio Alvarotti (Menato)." 6: Sambin, "I testamenti di Alvise Cornaro." *Italia Medioevale e Umanistica* 9 (1966): 229–385. Fundamental contributions to biography and understanding of cultural milieu.

Mortier, Alfred. *Un Dramaturge populaire de la Renaissance italienne Ruzzante*

(1502–1542). Paris: Peyronnet, 1925–26. First monograph on Beolco; many insights into Lovarini's discoveries; second volume contains French translations of most of the plays.

Oliveira Barata, Jose. "Sulla cultura del Ruzante." *Atti dell'Istituto Veneto di Scienze, Lettere ed Arti* (Classe di scienze morali, lettere ed arti) 131 (1972–73): 101–37. Analyzes Beolco's satire of humanistic orations; shows *The Cow Comedy* to be based on Renaissance translation, not Plautine original.

Padoan, Giorgio. "Angelo Beolco da Ruzante a Perduoçimo." In *Momenti del Rinascimento veneto*. Padua: Antenore, 1978. Gives evidence for dates of plays, links them with other literary works.

Prosperi, Mario. *Angelo Beolco nominato ruzante*. Padua: Liviana, 1970. Explores the religious dimension of Beolco's works; minimizes rebelliousness.

Puppa, Paolo. "Il contadino in Ruzante tra 'foira' carnevalesca e maschera sociale." In *Convegno internazionale di Studi sul Ruzante,* edited by Giovanni Calendoli and Giuseppe Vellucci, 149–79. Venice: Corbo e Fiore, 1987. Examines the changing tensions generated in Beolco's work by various opposing forces.

Radcliff-Umstead, Douglas. *The Birth of Modern Comedy in the Renaissance.* Chicago: University of Chicago Press, 1969. Section on Beolco notes connections of Beolco's late plays with formal literature.

Savarese, Nicola. "In morte di Angelo Beolco detto Ruzante: La *Canace* dello Speroni." *Biblioteca teatrale* 15–16 (1976): 170–91. Important assessment of Beolco's late career in light of cultural trends.

Ulysse, George. "La *Pastoral* del Ruzante e le egloghe pastorali e rusticali dei Pre-Rozzi Senesi." In *Convegno internazionale di Studi sul Ruzante,* edited by Giovanni Calendoli and Giuseppe Vellucci, 69–89. Venice: Corbo e Fiore, 1987. Compares Beolco's play with those of contemporary Sienese writers of rustic comedies; elucidates similarities and differences.

Index